AEROSHORTS COLLECTION
SIMPLE AVIATION

AeroShorts Collection - Simple Aviation

Author: Dustin Grüne
Publisher: This book is self-published by Dustin Grüne via Amazon KDP. Printed and distributed by Amazon KDP.
ISBN: 9798310938380

Disclaimer:

This book is for informational purposes only. The author and publisher have made every effort to ensure the accuracy of the information in this book. However, they assume no liability for any errors, omissions, or outcomes resulting from the use of this content. Readers should always verify critical aviation information with official sources, as regulations and procedures may vary by country and are subject to change.

© 2025 AeroShorts

All rights reserved. No part of this publication may be copied, reproduced, stored in a retrieval system, or transmitted in any form or by any means—electronic, mechanical, photocopying, recording, or otherwise—without the prior written permission of the publisher, except in the case of brief quotations for review purposes.

Dustin Grüne, c/o IP-Management #4010, Ludwig-Erhard-Str. 18, 20459 Hamburg

Introduction

Welcome to Simple Aviation, a journey into the fascinating world of aviation! This book is a culmination of my passion for flight and my desire to make complex aviation topics accessible to everyone. If you've watched my videos, you'll know that I strive to break down intricate concepts into simple, easy-to-understand explanations.

This book is no different—it's an extension of that mission, designed to take you deeper into the subjects we've explored together. From the science of flight to the intricacies of aircraft systems, navigation, and safety, this book covers a wide range of topics that are essential for anyone curious about aviation.

Whether you're an aspiring pilot, an aviation enthusiast, or simply someone who loves to learn, I hope this book will inspire and educate you. I want to take a moment to thank my incredible community—your support, curiosity, and engagement have been the driving force behind this project.

Your questions and feedback have shaped not only my videos but also this book. Thank you for being a part of this journey. So, fasten your seatbelt, and let's take off into the world of aviation together. I hope you enjoy reading this book as much as I enjoyed creating it!

FOLLOW AEROSHORTS ON SOCIAL MEDIA

Table of Contents

The Basics of Flight 9
    Aerodynamics 10
    Air Pressure 14
    Wind Shear 15
    The Ground Effect in Aviation 19
    Speeds in Aviation 22
    Understanding Turbulence 24
    Airplane Flight Controls 27
    Bank Angle 30
    Basic Traffic Pattern 32

Aircraft Anatomy and Systems 35
    Aircraft Engine Types 36
    Landing Gear 40
    Hydraulic Systems 40
    Aircraft Wings 44
    Aircraft Lights 48
    Pitot-Static-System 51
    Aircraft Window Design 53

Airport Infrastructure and Operations 57
    Runway Markings 58
    Runway Digits 60
    Essential Taxiway Markings and Signs 60
    How Windsocks Work 65
    PAPI Lights 67
    Understanding Airport Codes 70

Flight Instruments and Avionics 75
    6 PACK Aircraft Instruments 76
    Avionics - The Brain of the Aircraft 78
    Flight Envelope Protection Systems 81
    The Black Box 85
    GPS in Aviation 87
    Aircraft Transponders 89
    QNH, QFE & QNE 92

Navigation and Flight Management 97
    VOR Navigation 98
    Distance Measuring Equipment (DME) 101
    Non-Directional Beacon (NDB) 104
    ILS - (Instrument Landing System) 107
    RNAV and LNAV 108
    Vertical Navigation (VNAV) 111
    Standard Instrument Departures (SIDs) 114
    Standard Terminal Arrival Routes (STARs) 118
    Holdings 122
    True Heading vs. Magnetic Heading 126
    Navigation on Earth 129
    How a Flight Route is Structured 133
    FMS - Flight Management System 136

Meteorology for Aviators 139
    Layers of the Atmosphere 140
    Weather Fronts 143
    Understanding Weather Charts, NOTAMs, and TAFs 147
    METAR 152

Air Traffic Control and Communication 157
    ATC 158
    VFR & IFR 161
    Phraseology and Communication 164
    Understanding Airspace Classes 168
    TCAS - Traffic Collision Avoidance System 172

Safety and Operational Procedures 175
The Importance of Pre-Flight Checklists 176
SOPs - Standard Operating Procedures 178
Crew Resource Management (CRM) 181
Emergency Procedures and Management 184
ETOPS 188
Decision Altitude (DA) and Decision Height (DH) 191

Human Factors and Decision-Making 195
Human Factors in Aviation 196
Aircraft Fuel Systems 198
Environmental Control System (ECS) 201
Pressurization and Oxygen Systems 203
Deicing and Anti-Icing Systems 208

Environmental Impact and Innovations 213
Aviation and Climate Change 214
Introduction to Engine Chevrons 217
Why Airplanes Are Mostly White? 219

Pilot Training and Career Pathways 223
Steps to Becoming a Pilot 224
Networking in Aviation 230
Vocabulary 232

Special Topics and FAQs 237
Why Aircraft Lights are Dimmed During Takeoff & Landing? 238
Why Don't PLANES Have Parachutes for Passengers? 239
Aircraft Communication Systems 241

Chapter 1

The Basics of Flight

Aerodynamics

Aerodynamics is the study of the behavior of air as it interacts with solid objects, such as an airplane. Understanding the basics of aerodynamics is crucial for comprehending how airplanes achieve and maintain flight. This chapter will delve into the fundamental principles of aerodynamics, focusing on the forces at play and how they interact to enable flight.

The Four Forces of Flight

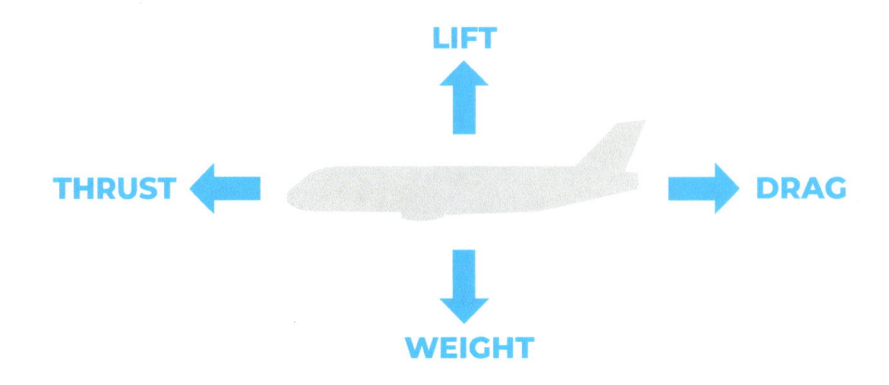

An aircraft in flight is influenced by four fundamental forces: **lift**, **weight**, **thrust**, and **drag**. Lift is generated by the wings and counteracts weight, which is the force of gravity pulling the aircraft downward. Thrust, produced by engines or propellers, propels the aircraft forward, overcoming drag, which is the resistance caused by air friction. For stable flight, these forces must be balanced, with lift equaling weight and thrust overcoming drag. Any change in these forces affects the aircraft's motion, requiring adjustments from the pilot or flight control systems.

Lift

Lift is the force that enables an airplane to rise off the ground and stay in the air. It is generated by the movement of the airplane's wings through the air. According to **Bernoulli's principle**, as air flows over the curved upper surface of the wing, it speeds up and its pressure decreases. The higher pressure below the wing compared to the lower pressure above creates an upward force. The shape of the wing, known as an airfoil, is specifically designed to optimize this pressure difference and maximize lift.

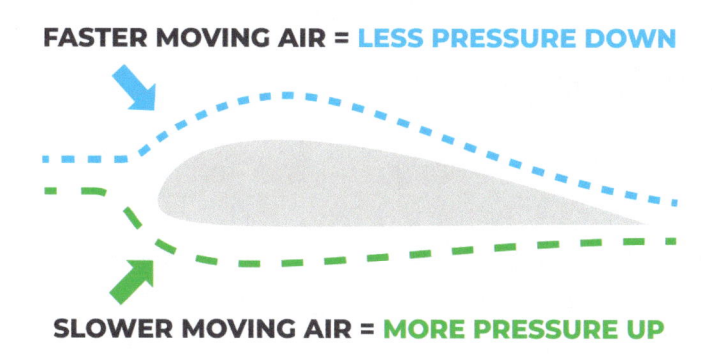

FASTER MOVING AIR = LESS PRESSURE DOWN

SLOWER MOVING AIR = MORE PRESSURE UP

Weight

Weight is the force caused by gravity pulling the airplane toward the Earth. It acts downward and must be counteracted by lift for the airplane to ascend and remain airborne. The airplane's weight includes everything on board, such as passengers, cargo, fuel, and the aircraft itself. Proper balance and distribution of weight are essential for stable flight.

Thrust

Thrust is the forward force produced by the airplane's engines. It propels the airplane through the air, allowing the wings to generate lift. In jet engines, thrust is created by expelling exhaust gases at high speed. In propeller-driven airplanes, thrust is generated by the rotation of the propeller blades pushing air backward. The amount of thrust must exceed drag for the airplane to accelerate and maintain flight.

Drag

Drag is the resistance force that opposes the airplane's motion through the air. It is caused by air friction and pressure differences as the airplane moves. There are two main types of drag: parasitic drag and induced drag. Parasitic drag includes form drag (**caused by the airplane's shape**), skin friction (**caused by the airplane's surface texture**), and interference drag (**caused by the interaction of various aircraft components**). Induced drag is a byproduct of lift and occurs when the wing generates lift, creating vortices at the wingtips that increase resistance.

Principles of Aerodynamics

Bernoulli's Principle

Bernoulli's principle states that an increase in the speed of a fluid (**in this case, air**) occurs simultaneously with a decrease in pressure. This principle explains how the curved shape of an airplane wing (**airfoil**) generates lift. As air flows over the curved upper surface of the wing, it accelerates and its pressure drops. The higher pressure beneath the wing compared to the lower pressure above creates an upward lifting force.

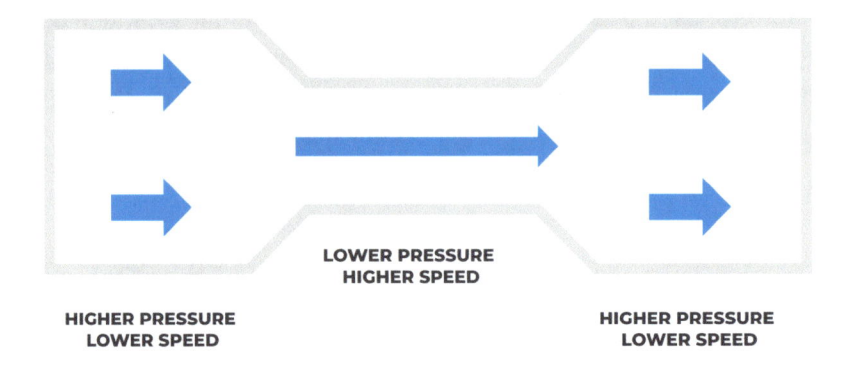

**LOWER PRESSURE
HIGHER SPEED**

**HIGHER PRESSURE
LOWER SPEED**

**HIGHER PRESSURE
LOWER SPEED**

The Basics of Flight

Newton's Third Law of Motion

Newton's third law states that for every action, there is an equal and opposite reaction. In the context of aerodynamics, this law is evident in how thrust is generated. For instance, when jet engines expel exhaust gases backward, the airplane is propelled forward with an equal and opposite force. Similarly, the wings push air downward, resulting in an upward lift force.

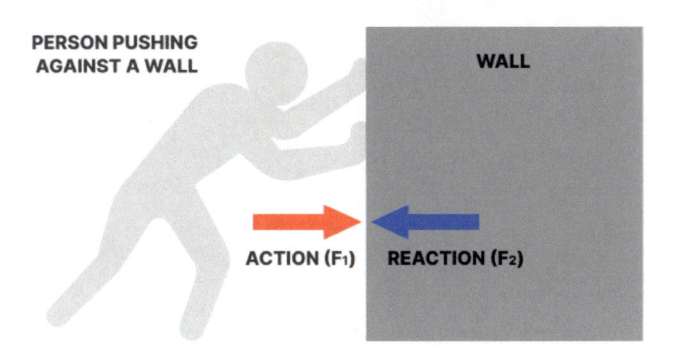

PERSON PUSHING AGAINST A WALL **WALL**

ACTION (F_1) **REACTION (F_2)**

F_1 Force applied by the person on the wall F_2 Force exerted by the wall on the person

Angle of Attack

The angle of attack is the angle between the wing's chord line (**an imaginary line from the leading to the trailing edge of the wing**) and the oncoming airflow. Adjusting the angle of attack changes the amount of lift generated. A higher angle of attack increases lift up to a certain point, but if the angle is too steep, it can lead to a stall, where airflow separation occurs, and lift dramatically decreases.

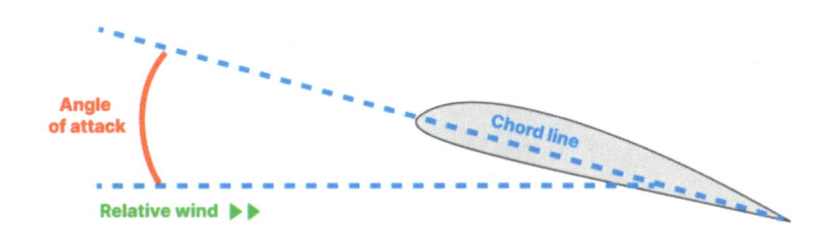

Angle of attack   **Chord line**

Relative wind ▶▶

The Basics of Flight | 13

Airfoil Shape

The shape of the airfoil is critical in determining how effectively a wing generates lift. The airfoil is typically designed with a curved upper surface and a flatter lower surface, creating the pressure differential needed for lift. Various airfoil shapes are optimized for different types of flight, such as high-speed flight, slow flight, or maneuverability.

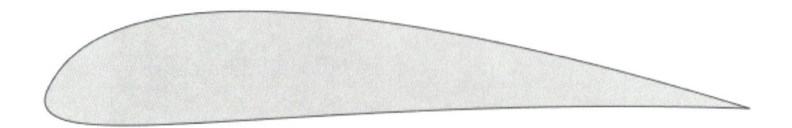

Air Pressure

In the realm of aviation, air pressure plays a fundamental role. It's the force exerted by air molecules on any surface they come into contact with. Imagine yourself standing at sea level, where the air pressure is at its highest. As you ascend to higher altitudes, such as atop a mountain, the air pressure decreases. This is because the higher you go, the fewer air molecules are present above you, exerting less force per unit area.

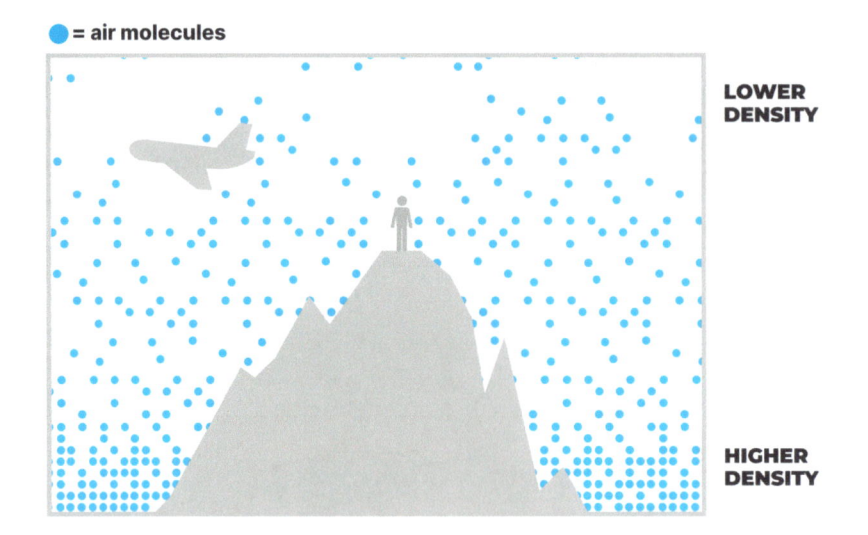

There are two primary types of air pressure we encounter:

Static Pressure

This is the pressure exerted by a fluid (**in this case, air**) when it's at rest. It remains constant around an aircraft at a specific altitude, regardless of its motion.

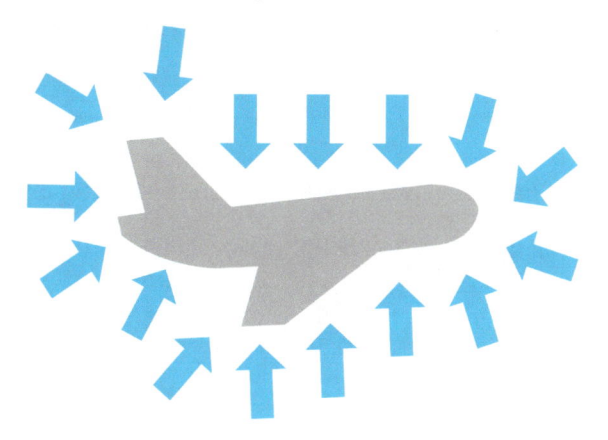

Dynamic Pressure

Unlike static pressure, dynamic pressure is the force exerted by a fluid in motion. It changes with the speed of the aircraft and is crucial in understanding aerodynamic forces.

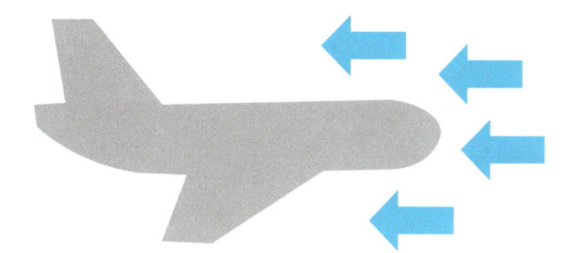

Wind Shear

Wind shear is a meteorological phenomenon that poses significant risks to aviation, particularly during critical phases of flight such as takeoff and landing. Sudden changes in wind speed and direction can disrupt an aircraft's flight path, challenging even the most experienced pilots. In this chapter, we will explore what wind shear is, how it affects aircraft, and why it is particularly dangerous during landing.

Understanding Wind Shear

Definition

Wind shear refers to the rapid change in wind speed and/or direction over a relatively short distance in the atmosphere. It can occur horizontally or vertically and is often associated with weather phenomena such as thunderstorms, temperature inversions, and frontal systems.

Types of Wind Shear

Horizontal Wind Shear: Changes in wind speed and direction along the horizontal plane.

Vertical Wind Shear: Changes in wind speed and direction along the vertical plane, which is particularly impactful during climb and descent.

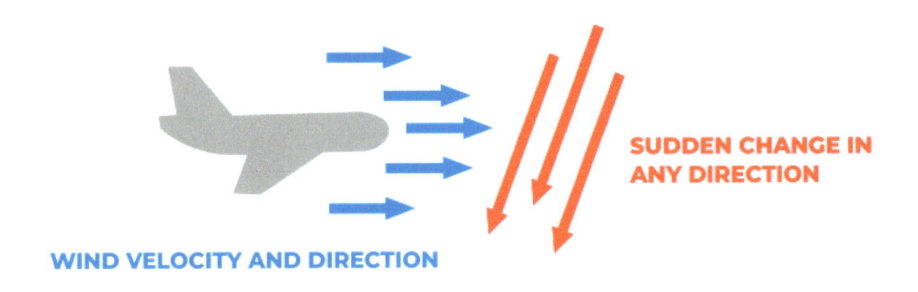

WIND VELOCITY AND DIRECTION

SUDDEN CHANGE IN ANY DIRECTION

Causes of Wind Shear

Thunderstorms

Thunderstorms are a common source of wind shear, especially in the vicinity of downdrafts and microbursts. These intense, localized bursts of wind can rapidly alter wind conditions around an aircraft.

Temperature Inversions

Temperature inversions, where a layer of warmer air sits above cooler air, can create sharp wind speed and direction gradients, leading to wind shear.

Frontal Systems

The boundaries between air masses of different temperatures, known as fronts, can generate wind shear as they move and interact.

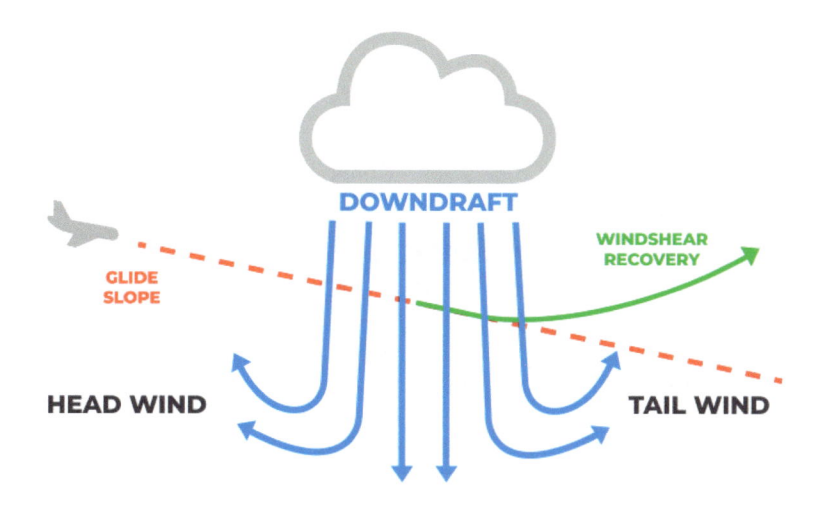

Impact on Aircraft During Landing:

Loss of Airspeed

A sudden shift from a headwind to a tailwind can cause a rapid **loss of airspeed**. During landing, maintaining airspeed is critical for control and stability. A sudden decrease can lead to a stall or an uncontrolled descent.

Altitude Variations

Wind shear can cause *abrupt changes in altitude*, making it challenging for pilots to maintain the correct glide path. This is particularly hazardous during landing when the aircraft is close to the ground and there is little room for error.

Increased Workload for Pilots

Pilots must make rapid and precise *adjustments* to control surfaces and engine power to counteract the effects of wind shear. The increased workload and stress can lead to pilot error, further complicating the landing process.

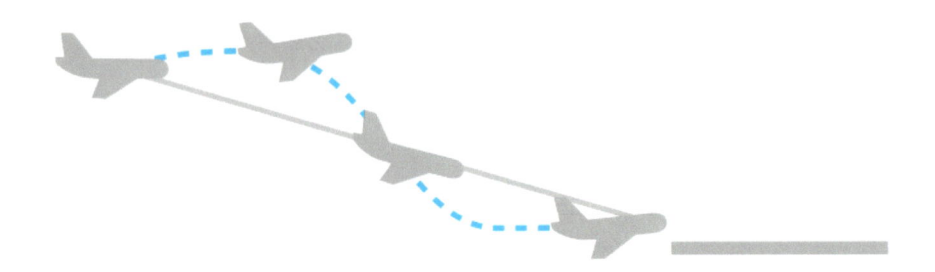

Wind Shear Detection Systems:

Onboard Wind Shear Detection Systems

Reactive Wind Shear Detection: Reactive systems, such as the **Ground Proximity Warning System (GPWS)**, alert pilots to the presence of wind shear only after the aircraft has already encountered it. These systems use inputs from the aircraft's sensors to detect rapid changes in wind speed and direction.

Predictive Wind Shear Detection: Predictive systems, like the **Predictive Wind Shear System (PWS),** provide advanced warning of potential wind shear ahead of the aircraft. Using Doppler radar technology, these systems detect wind shear conditions along the flight path and alert pilots, allowing them to take preemptive action.

Ground-Based Wind Shear Detection Systems

Low-Level Wind Shear Alert System (LLWAS): LLWAS consists of a network of ground-based sensors around airports that detect wind speed and direction changes. The system provides real-time alerts to air traffic controllers, who then inform pilots of potential wind shear conditions.

Terminal Doppler Weather Radar (TDWR): TDWR systems use Doppler radar technology to detect and monitor wind shear and microburst activity near airports. These systems provide detailed information on wind patterns and are particularly effective at identifying hazardous conditions during takeoff and landing.

The Ground Effect in Aviation

The **"ground effect"** is a phenomenon that affects the aerodynamics of an aircraft as it flies close to the ground. Understanding how this effect works is *crucial* for pilots, as it influences both takeoff and landing performance. This chapter explores what the ground effect is, how it occurs, and why it's important to recognize and manage it during flight.

What is Ground Effect?

The ground effect occurs when an aircraft is flying *within a wingspan's height* of the ground. In this region, the interaction between the airflow around the wings and the surface below causes changes in lift and drag. Specifically, the proximity to the ground alters the behavior of the airflow under the aircraft's wings, leading to a temporary increase in lift and a reduction in drag.

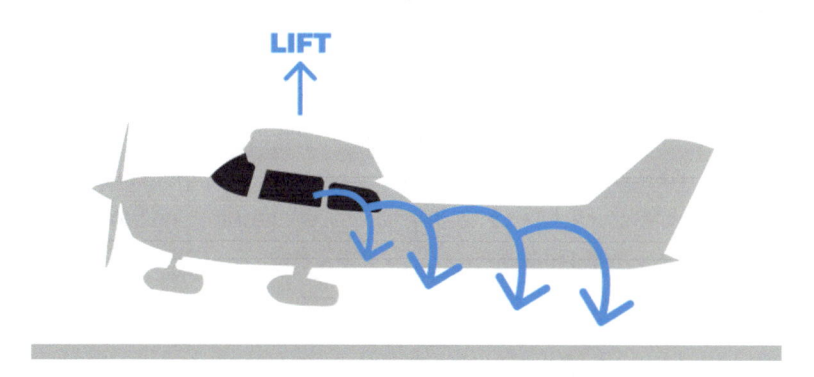

How Ground Effect Occurs

When an aircraft is flying at altitude, the wings create lift by deflecting air *downward*. This process produces a wake of turbulent air behind and beneath the aircraft. The downward movement of the air creates induced drag—a byproduct of the wing generating lift. However, as an aircraft flies close to the ground (**typically within one wingspan's height**), the ground interrupts the airflow pattern. This disturbance:

Reduces Wingtip Vortices: Wingtip vortices are swirling masses of air created at the tips of an aircraft's wings. They contribute significantly to induced drag. As the aircraft gets closer to the ground, the formation of these vortices is hindered, resulting in less induced drag.

Increases Lift Efficiency: The reduction in induced drag means the wings can generate more lift with less effort. Essentially, the aircraft's wings become more efficient at producing lift when flying near the ground.

The Basics of Flight

Effects of Ground Effect on Takeoff

During takeoff, pilots can experience ground effect when the aircraft is just lifting off the runway. As the airplane ascends and is within about one wingspan's height of the ground, the *increase in lift and reduction in drag* might cause the aircraft to feel as though it is flying more easily than at higher altitudes. This can lead to the sensation that the aircraft has enough speed to climb, even when it may not.

If a pilot attempts to climb too steeply while still under the influence of ground effect, the aircraft may lose lift suddenly as it rises out of this effect, causing it to sink back toward the runway. For this reason, it's important to gain sufficient airspeed before climbing out of ground effect to ensure safe and stable flight.

Effects of Ground Effect on Landing

During landing, ground effect can cause the airplane to "*float*" above the runway longer than expected. As the aircraft descends into ground effect, the *increased lift and reduced drag* can make it harder for the plane to descend at the expected rate. This can result in the aircraft remaining airborne for a longer period, delaying touchdown.

Pilots must account for this floating tendency, especially during flare (**the final moments before touchdown**), by adjusting the aircraft's attitude and managing speed carefully. Failing to anticipate ground effect can lead to an extended landing distance, which might be problematic if runway length is limited.

Factors that Influence Ground Effect

The strength of the ground effect depends on several factors:

Aircraft Size: The larger the wingspan of the aircraft, the more pronounced the ground effect will be. For smaller planes, such as light aircraft, the effect may still be noticeable but less extreme.

Height Above Ground: The ground effect is strongest when an aircraft is within a height of about one wingspan from the ground. It diminishes rapidly as the aircraft climbs higher. Beyond an altitude of roughly one wingspan, the effect is almost nonexistent.

Aircraft Configuration: The design of the aircraft, particularly the wing shape and size, will influence how strongly the ground effect is felt. Low-wing aircraft, for example, tend to experience more pronounced ground effect compared to high-wing aircraft because the wings are closer to the ground.

High Altitude Vortices

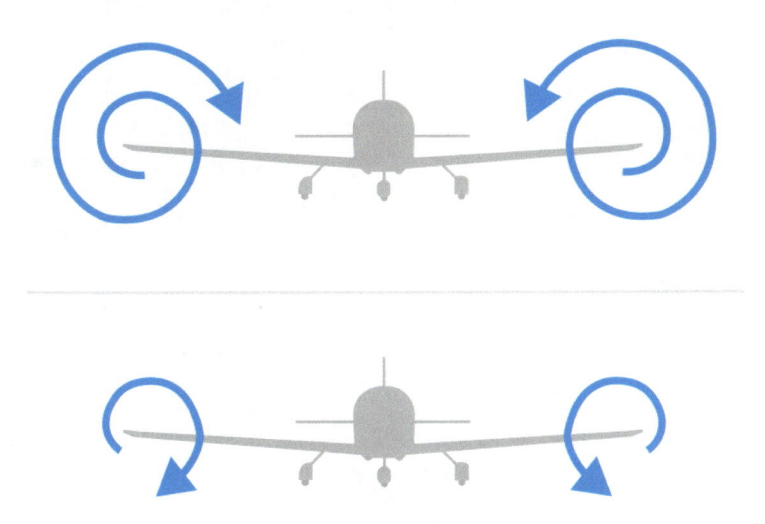

Low Altitude Vortices

Managing Ground Effect in Flight

Pilots need to be aware of the ground effect and manage it properly during takeoff and landing. Here are a few key considerations:

Takeoff: During takeoff, it's essential to wait until the aircraft reaches the appropriate climb speed before attempting to leave the ground effect zone. If the aircraft leaves ground effect too soon, it may experience a sudden loss of lift, causing it to sink. This can lead to a dangerous situation if the aircraft is still near the ground and lacks enough speed for a proper climb.

Landing: During landing, anticipate that ground effect may cause the aircraft to float above the runway. To avoid overshooting the landing point, reduce airspeed and manage descent carefully. Flaps can help by increasing drag and countering some of the extra lift caused by ground effect.

The Basics of Flight

The ground effect is a fascinating aerodynamic phenomenon that plays a significant role in flight, particularly during takeoff and landing. By understanding how it affects lift and drag near the ground, pilots can make informed decisions to ensure smooth and safe operations. While the ground effect can be advantageous by temporarily boosting lift and reducing drag, it can also present challenges if not managed correctly. Proper technique and awareness are essential to leveraging the benefits and mitigating the risks of the ground effect.

Speeds in Aviation

Understanding the various types of speeds in aviation is crucial for pilots and anyone interested in the intricacies of flight. Different speed measurements provide critical information about an aircraft's performance, navigation, and safety. This chapter will explore the primary speeds used in aviation, including True Airspeed (**TAS**), Ground Speed (**GS**), and others, explaining their definitions, importance, and applications.

Indicated Airspeed (IAS)

Definition: Indicated Airspeed (**IAS**) is the speed *shown on the aircraft's airspeed indicator*. It is the measure of dynamic pressure of the air flowing over the wings.

Importance: IAS is crucial for flight safety and performance. It helps pilots adhere to speed limits for specific phases of flight, such as takeoff, landing, and maneuvering. It is also used to determine stall speeds and to ensure structural limits are not exceeded.

Calibrated Airspeed (CAS)

Definition: Calibrated Airspeed (**CAS**) is IAS *corrected for instrument and position errors*.

Importance: CAS provides a more accurate speed reading than IAS, accounting for errors introduced by the airspeed indicator and its installation in the aircraft.

True Airspeed (TAS)

Definition: True Airspeed (**TAS**) is the actual speed of an aircraft relative to the air through which it is flying. TAS is *IAS corrected for altitude and non-standard temperature*.

Importance: TAS is vital for navigation and flight planning. It helps pilots determine how fast they are traveling over the ground when combined with wind speed and direction.

Ground Speed (GS)

Definition: Ground Speed (**GS**) is the *speed of an aircraft relative to the ground*. It is TAS adjusted for wind effects.

Importance: GS is essential for navigation, especially when estimating arrival times and fuel consumption. It directly affects how long a flight will take to reach its destination.

Mach Number (M)

Definition: Mach Number is the *ratio of an aircraft's speed to the speed of sound* in the surrounding air.

Importance: Mach Number is particularly important for high-speed and high-altitude flight, such as in jet aircraft and supersonic planes. It helps in avoiding the effects of shock waves and ensuring structural integrity at high speeds.

Vertical Speed (VS)

Definition: Vertical Speed (**VS**) is the *rate at which an aircraft ascends or descends*, usually measured in feet per minute (**fpm**).

Importance: VS is critical for maintaining desired climb or descent profiles and ensuring safe altitude changes, especially during takeoff and landing phases.

V-Speeds

Definition: V-Speeds are specific *airspeeds that define certain operational limits and performance characteristics of an aircraft*. They include a variety of speeds like V1 (**takeoff decision speed**), V2 (**takeoff safety speed**), and VNE (**never-exceed speed**).

Importance: V-Speeds are essential for safe aircraft operation, helping pilots make crucial decisions during takeoff, landing, and emergency situations. They are determined by the aircraft manufacturer and are based on extensive testing.

The various speeds in aviation, including **IAS**, **CAS**, **TAS**, **GS**, and **Mach Number**, each play a significant role in flight operations. They provide essential information for navigation, safety, performance, and flight planning. By understanding and correctly using these speeds, pilots can ensure efficient and safe flights, contributing to the overall success and safety of aviation operations. Whether you are a pilot, an aviation enthusiast, or a curious reader, grasping the basics of these speeds enriches your appreciation of the complexities involved in flying.

Understanding Turbulence

Turbulence is the irregular movement of air that aircraft encounter during flight. It's one of the most common phenomena in aviation and often misunderstood. While it can cause discomfort for passengers, turbulence is a normal and safe aspect of flying, thanks to the design and durability of modern aircraft.

In this chapter, we will explore the different types of turbulence, their causes, and why they are not a threat to flight safety.

Types of Turbulence

Turbulence can be categorized into several main types based on its cause and characteristics:

1. Clear Air Turbulence (CAT)

Definition: Turbulence occurring in clear skies without visible clouds or weather phenomena.

Cause: Differences in wind speed at high altitudes, often near jet streams.

Features:

- Difficult to detect visually or with onboard radar.
- Common at cruising altitudes.

Example: A sudden bump while flying at **35,000 feet**, even though the sky appears clear.

Clear Air Turbulence

2. Mechanical Turbulence

Definition: Turbulence caused by air flowing over uneven terrain, buildings, or other obstacles near the ground.

Cause: Air is disrupted by objects on the ground, creating eddies and irregular airflow.

Features:

- More common during takeoff and landing.
- Stronger in areas with mountains or tall structures.

Mechanical Turbulence

3. Wake Turbulence

Definition: Turbulence caused by the wingtip vortices of another aircraft.

Cause: Air spirals off the wingtips of an aircraft, creating a disturbance in the air.

Features:

- Stronger from larger aircraft, like the **Airbus A380** or **Boeing 747**.
- Avoided through proper spacing between aircraft.

The Basics of Flight | 25

Wake Turbulence

Why Is Turbulence Not Dangerous?

Turbulence might feel unsettling, but modern aircraft are designed to handle it safely. Here's why turbulence is not a threat:

1. Aircraft Durability

- Aircraft are built to withstand extreme forces far greater than those experienced in turbulence.
- Structural testing ensures that wings and other components remain intact even in severe turbulence.

2. Pilot Training

- Pilots are extensively trained to manage turbulence and know how to adjust flight paths or altitudes to minimize its impact.
- They use weather reports, radar, and communication with air traffic control to avoid turbulence whenever possible.

3. Automatic Systems

- Modern aircraft are equipped with autopilot systems that can adjust to turbulence, maintaining stability and minimizing sudden movements.

4. Turbulence Levels

- Most turbulence is mild or moderate. Severe turbulence is rare and does not pose a significant risk to the aircraft.

Turbulence is a natural part of flying and not something to fear. Understanding its causes and knowing that aircraft are designed to handle it can make your flight experience more reassuring. By staying informed and prepared, you can enjoy your journey through the skies with confidence.

Airplane Flight Controls

Flying an airplane might seem complex, but it all comes down to understanding its flight controls. These controls allow pilots to steer, climb, descend, and maintain stability during flight. Let's break it down step by step.

The Basics of Flight Controls

Flight controls are divided into primary controls and secondary controls:

1. Primary Flight Controls:

These are the essential controls that allow the airplane to move in three axes of motion:

- **Roll (Longitudinal Axis):** Movement of the wings up and down, controlled by the ailerons.
- **Pitch (Lateral Axis):** The airplane's nose moves up or down, controlled by the elevator or stabilator.
- **Yaw (Vertical Axis):** The airplane's nose moves left or right, controlled by the rudder.

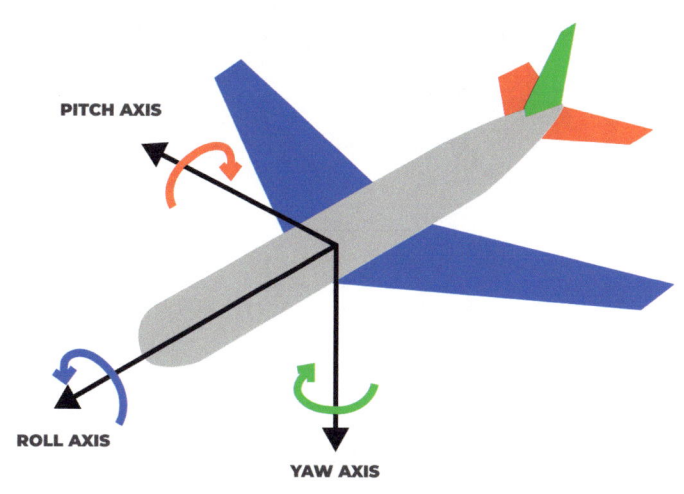

The Basics of Flight | 27

2. Secondary Flight Controls:

These assist the primary controls and improve efficiency and stability:

- **Flaps:** Increase lift or drag during takeoff and landing.
- **Spoilers:** Reduce lift and help slow the airplane.
- **Slats:** Located on the leading edge of the wing, slats improve airflow and allow the aircraft to fly at slower speeds without stalling.

How Each Control Works

Ailerons (Roll Control):

Found on the trailing edge of each wing, ailerons move in opposite directions. When one goes up, the other goes down. This creates a rolling motion, which helps the airplane turn.

Example: Turning left involves raising the right aileron (**reducing lift on the right wing**) and lowering the left aileron (**increasing lift on the left wing**).

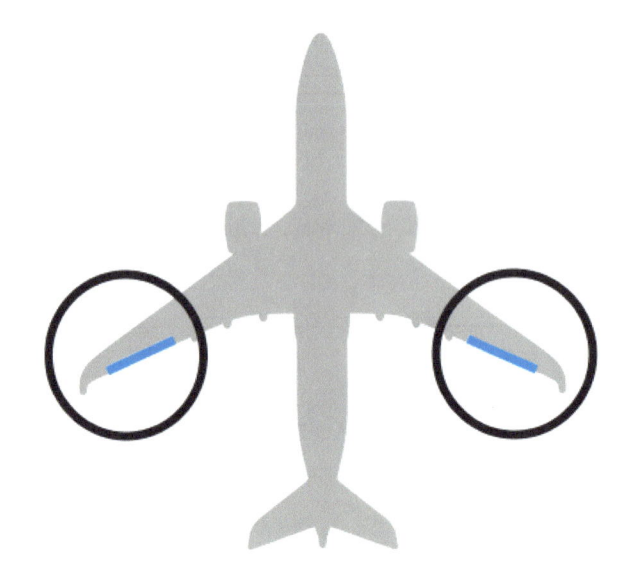

28 | The Basics of Flight

Elevator or Stabilator (Pitch Control):

Located on the tail (**horizontal stabilizer**), the elevator controls the airplane's nose. Pulling the control yoke back raises the elevator, causing the nose to go up (**climb**). Pushing the yoke forward lowers the elevator, making the nose go down (**descend**).

Rudder (Yaw Control):

Found on the tail (**vertical stabilizer**), the rudder is controlled by pedals in the cockpit. Pressing the right pedal moves the nose to the right, while pressing the left pedal moves it to the left. The rudder is especially important during turns and crosswind landings.

Secondary Flight Controls in Detail

Flaps

Flaps extend downward from the wing's trailing edge. They increase the wing's surface area, providing more lift at lower speeds. This is crucial during takeoff (**shorter distance required**) and landing (**steeper descent without increasing speed**).

Slats

Located on the leading edge of the wings, slats extend forward to allow smoother airflow over the wing at higher angles of attack, reducing the risk of a stall.

Spoilers

Found on the top of the wing, spoilers disrupt airflow, reducing lift. They are used during landings to help slow the airplane or during steep descents.

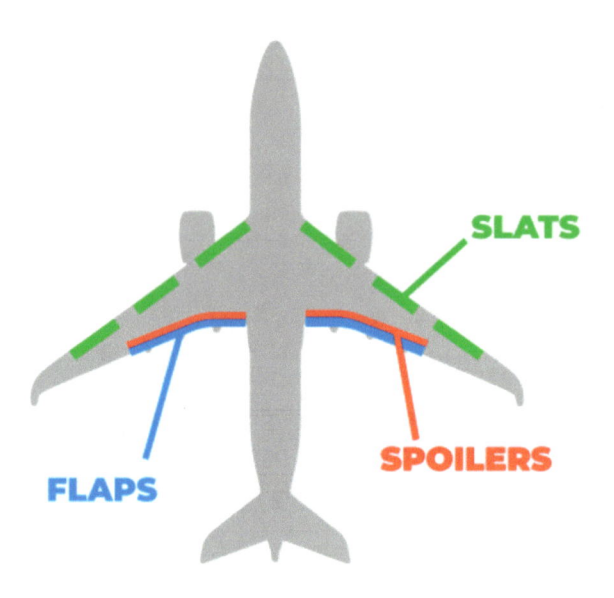

Bank Angle

In aviation, the bank angle is a crucial concept that refers to the tilt of an aircraft's wings relative to the horizon. This tilt occurs when an aircraft turns and is essential for controlling the direction of flight. Understanding bank angle helps pilots execute safe and efficient turns, maintain stability, and ensure passenger comfort.

Definition and Measurement

The bank angle is measured in degrees from the horizontal plane. When an aircraft banks, one wing dips lower than the other, creating a tilt that allows the aircraft to change its direction. The angle is typically measured using the aircraft's attitude indicator or turn coordinator.

LIFT

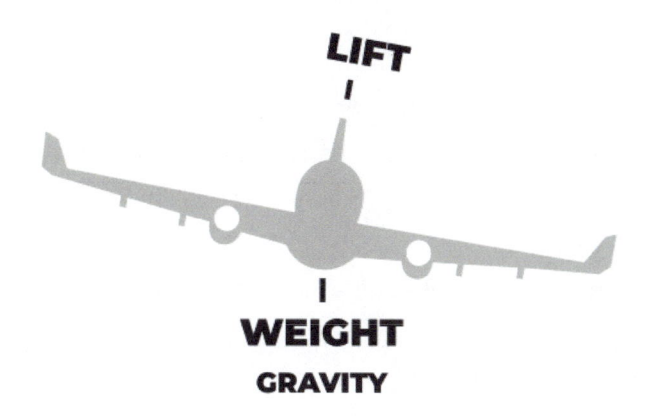

WEIGHT
GRAVITY

Importance of Bank Angle

Turning: To make a turn, an aircraft must bank to generate the *necessary* horizontal component of lift that pulls the aircraft into the turn. The greater the bank angle, the sharper the turn.

Stability and Control: Properly managing the bank angle is vital for maintaining *aircraft stability*. Excessive bank angles can lead to increased load factors and potential loss of control, while insufficient bank angles result in wide, inefficient turns.

Passenger Comfort: Smooth and gradual banking minimizes the forces felt by passengers, enhancing comfort during the flight. Sudden or steep banks can cause discomfort or alarm.

Calculating the Bank Angle for a Standard Turn

A standard turn in aviation is defined as a turn that results in a rate of 3 degrees per second. For a standard-rate turn, the bank angle can be approximated using the formula:

$$\text{Bank Angle} = \text{TAS} / 10 + 7$$

Where TAS is the True Airspeed of the aircraft in knots. This formula provides a practical estimate for pilots to achieve a standard-rate turn.

The Basics of Flight

Factors Affecting Bank Angle

Several factors influence the appropriate bank angle for a turn:

Airspeed: Higher speeds require shallower bank angles for the same rate of turn due to the increased radius of the turn. Conversely, lower speeds require steeper bank angles.

Aircraft Type: Different aircraft have varying limits on maximum permissible bank angles. These limits are defined in the aircraft's operating manual and must be adhered to for safety.

Load Factor: The load factor, or G-force, increases with bank angle. At a 60-degree bank, the load factor doubles, meaning the wings must support twice the aircraft's weight. Excessive load factors can lead to structural stress or failure.

Managing Bank Angle

Pilots must carefully manage bank angles to ensure safe and efficient flight operations. Here are some key practices:

Smooth Inputs: Gradual and smooth control inputs help maintain stability and prevent abrupt changes in bank angle.

Monitoring Instruments: Consistently monitoring the attitude indicator, turn coordinator, and other relevant instruments helps pilots maintain the desired bank angle and turn rate.

Adhering to Limits: Pilots must always respect the maximum bank angle limits specified for their aircraft to avoid overstressing the structure and ensure passenger safety.

Basic Traffic Pattern

In aviation, understanding the basic traffic pattern is crucial for safe and efficient flight operations, particularly at uncontrolled airports. The traffic pattern is a standardized path that aircraft follow when taking off, landing, or performing touch-and-go operations. It helps ensure that all pilots operating at or near an airport maintain situational awareness and avoid collisions. Here's an overview of the basic traffic pattern:

Components of the Traffic Pattern

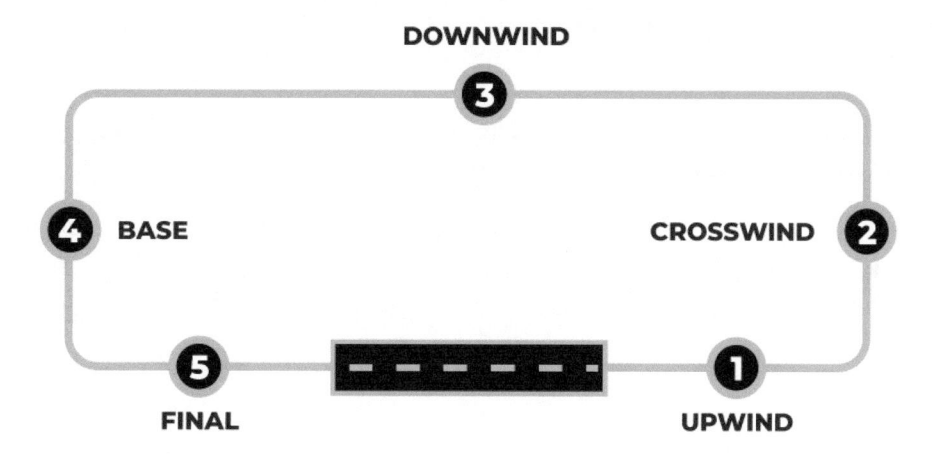

Upwind Leg (1)

This is the initial segment of the traffic pattern. After taking off, the aircraft climbs straight ahead along the runway heading. This leg is typically flown at full power as the plane gains altitude.

Crosswind Leg (2)

Once the aircraft reaches a safe altitude, usually *around 500 feet* above ground level (**AGL**), the pilot makes a *90-degree turn* to the left or right (**depending on the pattern direction**) to enter the crosswind leg. This segment is perpendicular to the runway.

Downwind Leg (3)

Following the crosswind leg, the pilot makes *another 90-degree turn* in the same direction to enter the downwind leg. This leg runs parallel to the runway but in the opposite direction of landing. During this leg, the aircraft maintains a consistent altitude and speed, typically at the traffic pattern altitude, which is usually *around 1,000 feet AGL*.

Base Leg (4)

Upon reaching the appropriate distance from the runway threshold, the pilot makes a third *90-degree turn* to enter the base leg. This segment is perpendicular to the runway and prepares the aircraft for its final approach.

Final Leg (5)

The final leg is a 90-degree turn from the base leg, aligning the aircraft with the runway for landing. During this leg, the pilot makes any necessary adjustments to the descent rate and speed to ensure a smooth and safe landing.

The standard traffic pattern is typically flown *with all turns made to the left*. This is referred to as a left-hand traffic pattern.

However, some airports use right-hand traffic patterns *(**Non Standard Traffic Pattern**)* due to terrain, noise abatement procedures, or other considerations. Pilots must always check the airport's published procedures and NOTAMs (**Notices to Airmen**) for the correct traffic pattern direction.

Key Considerations

Altitude and Speed: Maintaining a consistent altitude and speed throughout the traffic pattern is essential for collision avoidance and efficient traffic flow.

Communication: At controlled airports, pilots must follow the instructions of air traffic controllers. At uncontrolled airports, pilots should announce their position and intentions on the common traffic advisory frequency (**CTAF**) to alert other pilots in the area.

Visual Scanning: Pilots must continuously scan for other aircraft throughout the traffic pattern to ensure safe separation and avoid conflicts.

The traffic pattern provides a predictable environment where pilots can safely sequence their aircraft for landing and takeoff. By following the established pattern, pilots can maintain situational awareness, anticipate the movements of other aircraft, and reduce the risk of mid-air collisions.

In summary, the basic traffic pattern is a fundamental aspect of aviation that ensures safe and orderly operations around airports. Understanding and adhering to the traffic pattern is essential for all pilots, whether they are flying solo or with others in the vicinity.

Chapter 2

Aircraft Anatomy and Systems

Aircraft Engine Types

Aircraft engines are the heart of any airplane. They provide the thrust needed to overcome drag and keep the aircraft flying. In this chapter, we will explore three primary types of jet engines: **Turbojet**, **Turbofan**, and **Turboprop**. Each type has unique features, advantages, and specific uses in aviation.

Turbojet Engines

What is a Turbojet?

A turbojet engine is the simplest type of jet engine. It works by compressing air, mixing it with fuel, igniting the mixture, and expelling the hot gases at high speed through a nozzle. This creates thrust to propel the aircraft.

How It Works

Intake: Air is drawn into the engine.

Compression: The air is compressed by a series of rotating blades in the compressor.

Combustion: Fuel is added and ignited, producing high-temperature and high-pressure gases.

Exhaust: The gases are expelled through a nozzle, creating thrust.

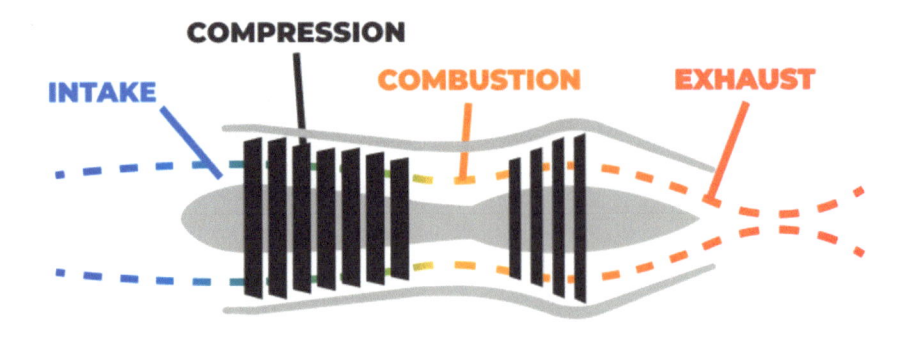

Key Features

High Speed: Turbojets are designed for high-speed flight, making them ideal for military jets and supersonic aircraft.

Efficiency: They are most efficient at high altitudes and speeds above Mach 1.

Noise: Turbojets are relatively loud because they expel gases at very high speeds.

Applications

- Military aircraft like fighter jets.
- Older commercial airliners, such as the Boeing 707 and the Concorde.

Turbofan Engines

What is a Turbofan?

A turbofan engine is an advanced version of the turbojet. It has a large fan at the front that pushes additional air around the engine core, producing extra thrust and improving fuel efficiency.

How It Works

Fan: A large fan draws in air. Some air goes into the core (**like a turbojet**), and the rest bypasses the core.

Core: The core functions like a turbojet, compressing and igniting air and fuel.

Bypass Air: The bypass air mixes with the exhaust gases to create additional thrust.

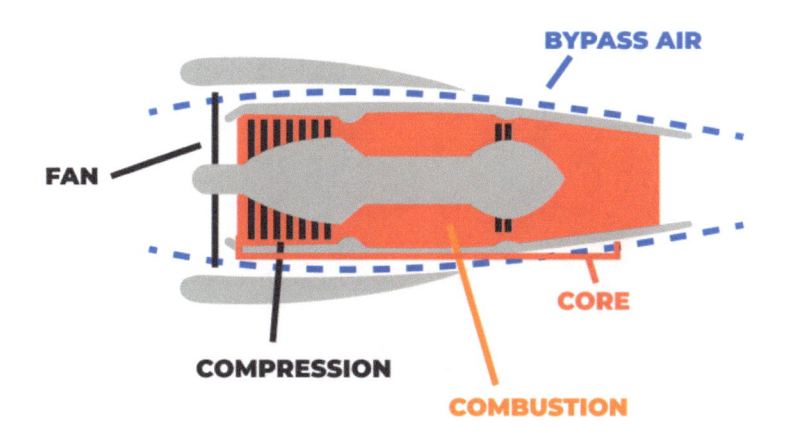

Key Features

High Efficiency: Turbofans are more fuel-efficient than turbojets, especially at subsonic speeds.

Quiet Operation: The bypass air reduces noise, making turbofans quieter.

Bypass Ratio: Turbofans are classified by their bypass ratio (**amount of bypass air vs. core air**). Higher bypass ratios mean better efficiency.

Applications

- Modern commercial airliners, like the **Boeing 737**, **A320**, and **Boeing 787**.
- Some military aircraft.

Turboprop Engines

What is a Turboprop?

A turboprop engine uses a jet engine to drive a propeller. Instead of producing thrust through high-speed exhaust gases, most of the power is transferred to the propeller for propulsion.

How It Works

Intake and Core: The engine core works similarly to a turbojet.

Power Turbine: A turbine extracts energy from the exhaust gases and transfers it to the propeller shaft.

Propeller: The propeller generates most of the thrust by moving a large volume of air at lower speeds.

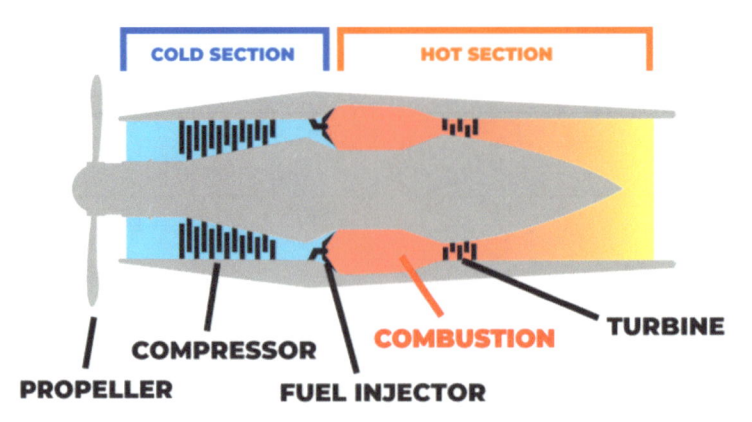

Key Features

Fuel Efficiency: Turboprops are extremely efficient at lower speeds and altitudes.

Short Runways: They perform well on shorter runways, making them ideal for regional and remote operations.

Lower Speed: Turboprops are slower than turbojets and turbofans, with cruising speeds around 300-400 knots.

Applications

- Regional airliners, like the **ATR 72** and **Bombardier Dash 8**.
- General aviation and small commuter aircraft.
- Military reconnaissance and cargo planes.

Comparison of Turbojet, Turbofan, and Turboprop

Feature	Turbojet	Turbofan	Turboprop
Thrust Generation	High-speed exhaust	Combination of fan and core	Propeller
Fuel Efficiency	Low at subsonic speeds	High at subsonic speeds	Highest at low speeds
Speed	Very high	Moderate to high	Lower
Noise	Loud	Quieter	Quietest
Best Use	Supersonic/military	Commercial airliners	Regional/ short-haul

Aircraft Anatomy and Systems

Landing Gear

As an aircraft descends towards the runway, the landing gear plays a *crucial role* in ensuring a safe touchdown and smooth deceleration. The landing gear system comprises various components designed to support the weight of the aircraft during landing, provide stability during ground operations, and withstand the forces encountered upon touchdown. In this chapter, we will explore the anatomy, operation, and importance of landing gear in aviation.

Anatomy of Landing Gear:

Main Landing Gear

The main landing gear is located *beneath the fuselage or wings of the aircraft* and typically consists of **wheels**, **shock absorbers**, and **struts**. These components bear the majority of the aircraft's weight during landing and support it during taxiing on the ground.

Nose Landing Gear

In tricycle landing gear configurations, a nose landing gear is located at the *front of the aircraft*. It typically consists of a **single wheel**, **shock absorber**, and **steering mechanism**. The nose landing gear assists in steering the aircraft during ground operations and supports the weight of the aircraft's forward section.

Retraction Mechanism

Many modern aircraft feature retractable landing gear systems that can be retracted into the fuselage or wings during flight *to reduce drag and improve aerodynamic performance*. The retraction mechanism comprises hydraulic or electric actuators that raise and lower the landing gear as commanded by the pilot.

Hydraulic Systems

Hydraulic systems are crucial components in modern aircraft, responsible for powering various control surfaces, landing gear, brakes, and other essential systems. Understanding the basics of aircraft hydraulics is essential for pilots to ensure the safe and efficient operation of their aircraft. This chapter will delve into the principles, components, and maintenance of hydraulic systems.

Introduction to Hydraulic Systems

Hydraulics is the technology of *controlling pressurized fluid* to generate, control, and transmit power. Aircraft hydraulic systems utilize *incompressible fluid*, **typically oil**, to transfer force from one location to another. This technology is favored in aviation due to its reliability, precision, and the ability to produce high power with relatively low weight.

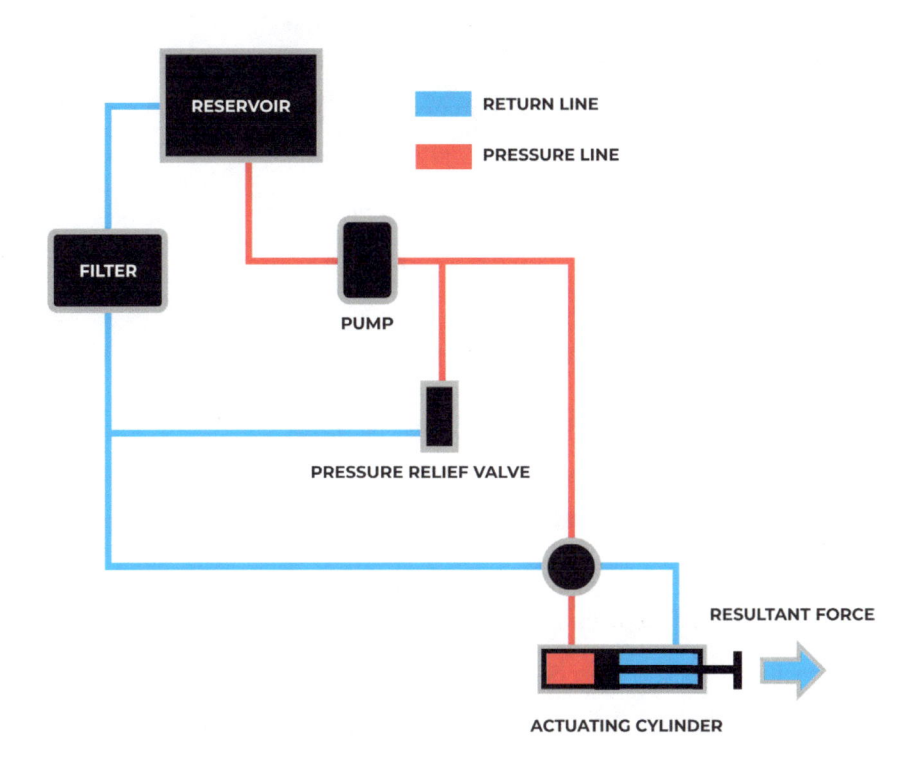

Principles of Hydraulics

The fundamental principle of hydraulics is Pascal's Law, which states that pressure applied to a confined fluid is transmitted equally in all directions. This allows hydraulic systems to amplify force and move heavy components with precision.

Key Concepts:

Pressure: Force exerted per unit area, typically measured in pounds per square inch (**PSI**) or bar.

Flow Rate: The volume of fluid that moves through a system in a given period, affecting the speed of actuator movement.

Force: Generated by pressure applied over an area, crucial for moving aircraft components.

Aircraft Anatomy and Systems | 41

Components of Hydraulic Systems

Aircraft hydraulic systems comprise several key components, each playing a vital role in the system's functionality.

Hydraulic Fluid:

- Acts as the medium for power transmission.
- Must have properties such as low compressibility, high lubricity, and stability across temperature ranges.
- Common fluids include MIL-H-5606, Skydrol, and HyJet.

Pumps:

- Convert mechanical energy into hydraulic energy.
- Types include gear pumps, piston pumps, and vane pumps.
- Often engine-driven or electrically powered.

Actuators

- Convert hydraulic energy back into mechanical motion.
- Types include hydraulic cylinders and hydraulic motors.
- Used in flight control surfaces, landing gear, and cargo doors.

Reservoirs

- Store hydraulic fluid and maintain a supply for the system.
- Allow for thermal expansion and aeration.

Valves

- Control the flow and pressure of hydraulic fluid.
- Types include check valves, relief valves, and selector valves.
- Ensure fluid flows in the desired direction and maintains safe pressure levels.

Accumulators

- Store hydraulic energy and smooth out pressure fluctuations.
- Can be gas-charged or spring-loaded.

Operation of Hydraulic Systems

Hydraulic systems operate through a series of steps involving the movement and control of hydraulic fluid:

Pump Activation: The hydraulic pump, driven by the aircraft engine or an electric motor, pressurizes the hydraulic fluid.

Fluid Distribution: Pressurized fluid is routed through lines and valves to various actuators.

Actuator Movement: Hydraulic actuators convert the fluid's pressure into mechanical motion, moving control surfaces, landing gear, etc.

Return to Reservoir: Used fluid returns to the reservoir for recirculation.

Maintenance of Hydraulic Systems

Proper maintenance of hydraulic systems is critical for ensuring reliability and safety.

Regular Inspections:

- Check for leaks, wear, and contamination.
- Inspect hoses, seals, and fittings for integrity.

Fluid Maintenance:

- Regularly monitor and replace hydraulic fluid.
- Test for contamination and fluid properties.

System Testing:

- Perform functional tests to verify the operation of pumps, actuators, and valves.
- Use ground support equipment for comprehensive system checks.

Common Issues and Troubleshooting

Leaks

- Identify and repair leaks promptly to prevent system failure.
- Common leak points include seals, hoses, and connections.

Contamination

- Contaminated fluid can cause wear and malfunction of components.
- Use filters and regular fluid analysis to prevent contamination.

Pressure Loss

- Check for issues with pumps, valves, or actuators if pressure is insufficient.
- Inspect for internal leaks or obstructions in the system.

Aircraft Wings

The wings of an aircraft are marvels of engineering, designed to provide lift, stability, and control during flight. They are not just simple surfaces but are equipped with various components that play crucial roles in the overall performance of the aircraft. In this chapter, we will explore the different parts of an aircraft wing and their functions.

Flaps

They are used to increase the lift of the wing during takeoff and landing. By extending the flaps, the wing area is increased, and the camber (**curvature**) of the wing is altered, allowing the aircraft to fly at slower speeds without stalling.

Slats

They work in conjunction with the flaps to enhance lift at lower speeds. When deployed, slats create a gap between themselves and the wing, allowing smooth airflow over the wing and delaying the stall.

Ailerons

They control the roll of the aircraft, which is the rotation around the longitudinal axis. When the pilot moves the control yoke or stick to the left or right, the ailerons move in opposite directions (**one up, one down**), causing the aircraft to roll in the desired direction.

Spoilers

They are used to reduce lift and increase drag. When deployed, spoilers disrupt the smooth airflow over the wing, causing a loss of lift and helping to slow down the aircraft, particularly during landing or descent.

Winglets

They improve the aerodynamic efficiency of the wing by reducing drag caused by wingtip vortices. This leads to better fuel efficiency and improved performance.

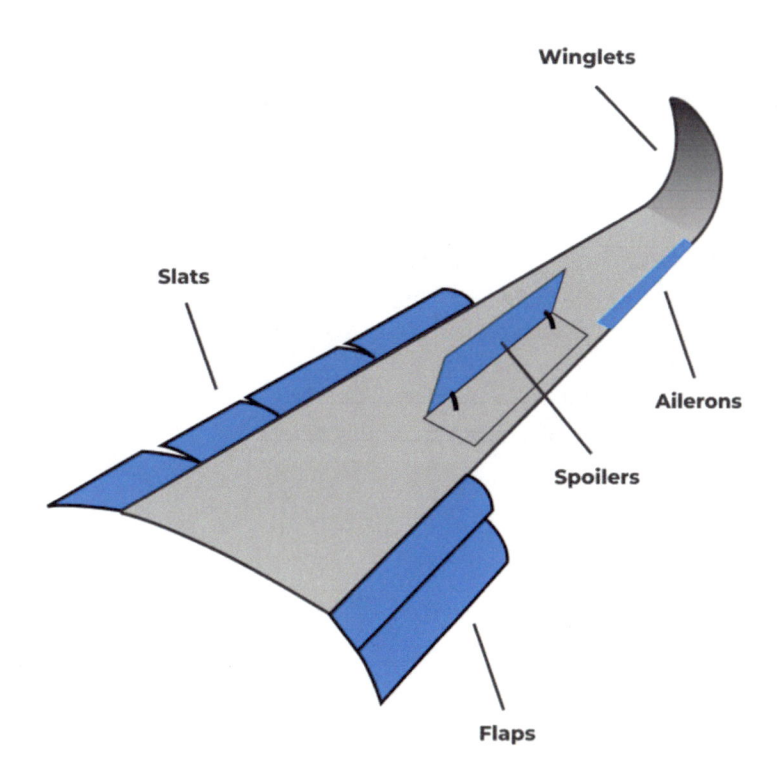

Aircraft Anatomy and Systems | 45

Some Wing Types

Straight Wings

Straight wings extend out from the fuselage at a right angle and are typically found on slower aircraft, such as small general aviation planes and older military aircraft.

Advantages: They provide good lift at low speeds and are easier to manufacture.

Disadvantages: They create more drag at higher speeds, limiting the aircraft's performance.

Swept Wings

Swept wings angle backward from the fuselage, commonly seen on modern jetliners and high-speed military aircraft.

Advantages: They reduce drag at high speeds and delay the onset of shockwaves as the aircraft approaches the speed of sound.

Disadvantages: They are less efficient at low speeds, requiring higher takeoff and landing speeds.

Delta Wings

Delta wings are triangular in shape and extend from the fuselage in a broad sweep.

Advantages: They provide high lift and stability at high speeds and are structurally strong.

Disadvantages: They have a higher drag at low speeds and can be more challenging to control during landing.

Canard Wings

Canard wings are small forewings placed near the nose of the aircraft, with the main wings positioned farther back.

Advantages: They provide additional lift and improve maneuverability and stall characteristics.

Disadvantages: They can create additional drag and complicate the aircraft's design and stability.

Variable-Sweep Wings

Also known as swing wings, these wings can change their angle of sweep in flight, seen in aircraft like the *F-14 Tomcat*.

Advantages: They offer the benefits of both straight and swept wings, allowing for efficient flight at various speeds.

Disadvantages: The mechanical complexity adds weight and maintenance requirements.

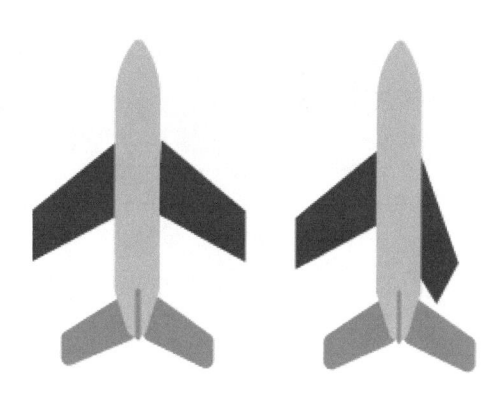

Aircraft Anatomy and Systems

Aircraft Lights

Aircraft lights play a crucial role in aviation, serving various purposes ranging from safety and navigation to communication. They help pilots see and be seen by others, both in the air and on the ground. This chapter will explore the different types of aircraft lights, their functions, and their importance in ensuring safe flight operations.

Types of Aircraft Lights and Their Functions:

Navigation Lights (Position Lights)

Function: Navigation lights are used to indicate the position and orientation of an aircraft to other pilots, especially at night. They help determine the direction the aircraft is facing.

Description: These lights are usually red, green, and white. The red light is located on the left (**port**) wingtip, the green light on the right (**starboard**) wingtip, and the white light on the tail. The position of these lights allows other pilots to determine the aircraft's heading and orientation in the dark.

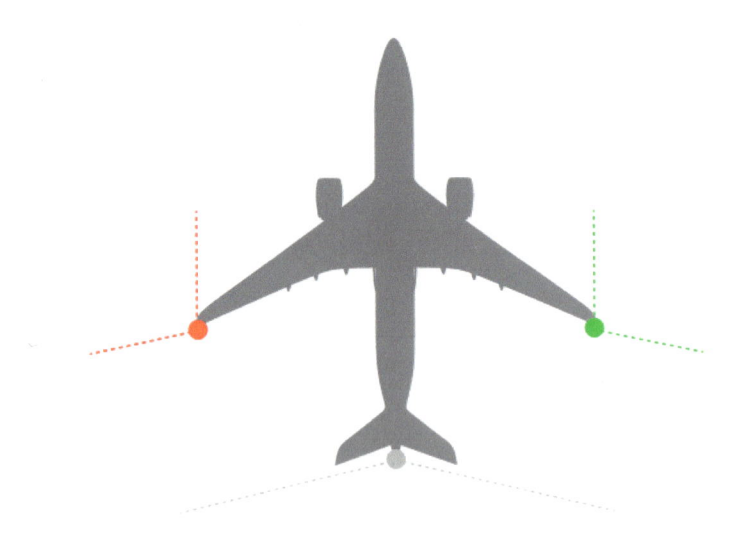

Beacon Lights (Anti-Collision Lights)

Function: Beacon lights are used to alert ground personnel and other pilots that the aircraft's engines are running or about to start. They enhance visibility and indicate that the aircraft is active.

Description: These are red rotating or flashing lights, typically mounted on the top and bottom of the fuselage. They are turned on before engine start and remain on until the engines are shut down.

Strobe Lights

Function: Strobe lights serve as anti-collision lights, making the aircraft more visible during flight, particularly in poor visibility conditions or at night.

Description: Strobe lights are high-intensity white flashing lights located on the wingtips and sometimes on the tail. They are extremely bright and can be seen from miles away, helping to prevent mid-air collisions.

Aircraft Anatomy and Systems

Landing Lights

Function: Landing lights are used to illuminate the runway during takeoff and landing, enhancing the pilot's visibility of the ground and other obstacles.

Description: These lights are typically located on the aircraft's nose, wing, or landing gear struts. They are powerful and project a concentrated beam of light forward, similar to the headlights of a car.

Taxi Lights

Function: Taxi lights are used to illuminate the taxiway during ground operations, helping pilots navigate the taxiways safely.

Description: These lights are usually mounted on the nose gear or the lower fuselage and provide a broad beam of light to illuminate the path ahead of the aircraft while it is taxiing.

Runway Turnoff Lights

Function: Runway turnoff lights provide additional illumination for turns off the runway onto taxiways, aiding in safe ground maneuvering.

Description: These lights are usually located on the wing roots or the lower fuselage and project light to the sides of the aircraft to illuminate the area where the aircraft will turn.

Aircraft lights are an integral part of aviation, playing a vital role in ensuring safety, aiding in navigation, and facilitating communication. From the basic position lights that help pilots orient themselves to the powerful landing lights that illuminate the runway, each type of light has a specific function that contributes to the smooth and safe operation of aircraft. Understanding these lights and their purposes enhances our appreciation of the complexities involved in modern aviation.

Pitot-Static-System

Now, let's shift our focus to the Pitot-Static System, a sophisticated setup designed to measure these pressures and provide crucial data to pilots during flight.

Pitot Tube

This ingenious device protrudes into the airstream, capturing the total pressure of the airflow. It's designed to face directly into the oncoming air, measuring both static and dynamic pressures.

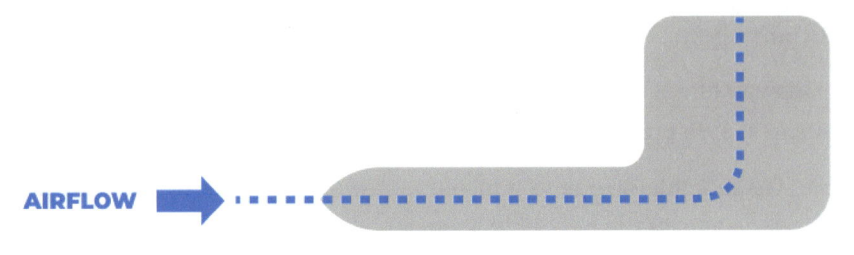

Pitot Tube

Static Port

Positioned perpendicular to the airflow, the static port measures only the static pressure of the undisturbed air surrounding the aircraft.

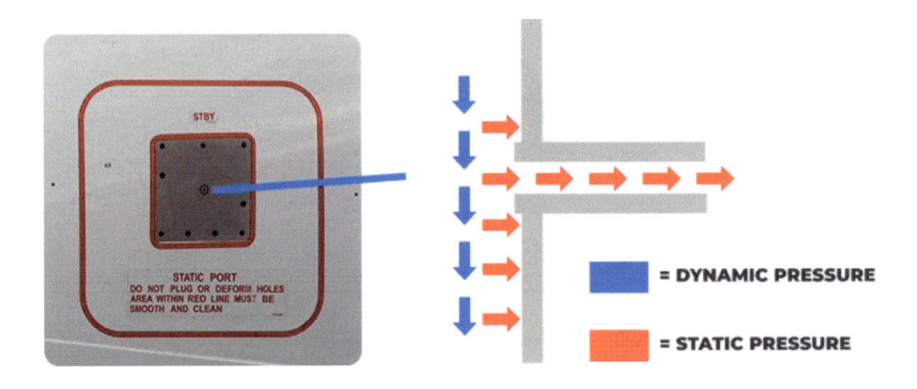

= DYNAMIC PRESSURE

= STATIC PRESSURE

The Pitot-Static System plays a pivotal role in flight instrumentation. By comparing the total pressure from the Pitot tube with the static pressure from the static port, onboard instruments like the airspeed indicator, altimeter, and vertical speed indicator provide accurate readings of airspeed, altitude, and climb/descent rates.

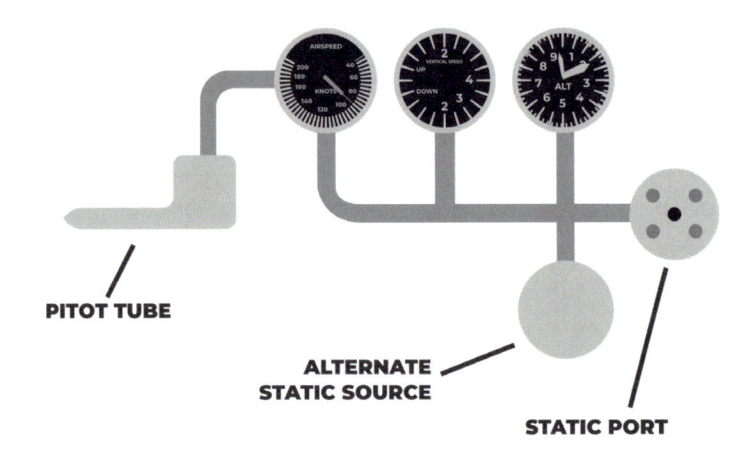

PITOT TUBE

ALTERNATE STATIC SOURCE

STATIC PORT

52 | **Aircraft Anatomy and Systems**

ADC (Air Data Computer)

The Role of the Air Data Computer (**ADC**): In modern aircraft, the data collected by the Pitot-Static System is further processed and analyzed by the Air Data Computer (**ADC**). This sophisticated onboard computer takes the raw pressure measurements and calculates various parameters such as true airspeed, Mach number, altitude, and air density. The ADC then feeds this processed information to other avionics systems for display to the pilot and for use in flight control systems.

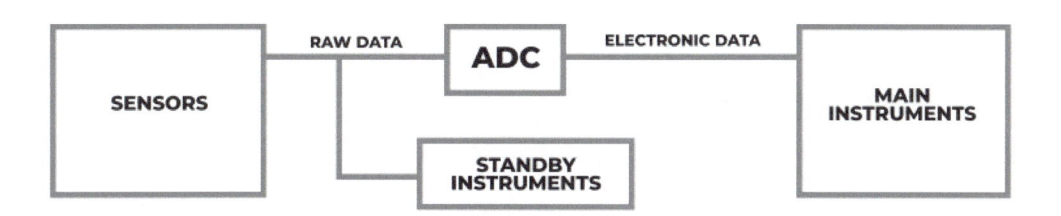

```
SENSORS --RAW DATA--> ADC --ELECTRONIC DATA--> MAIN INSTRUMENTS
                       |
                       v
                  STANDBY INSTRUMENTS
```

Aircraft Window Design

Aircraft windows are a crucial component of any aircraft, providing a view of the outside world while ensuring the safety and comfort of passengers. Their design is meticulously engineered to withstand the unique challenges of high-altitude flight, including changes in pressure, temperature, and wind. In this chapter, we will explore why aircraft windows have small holes and the three layers that make up an aircraft window.

The Purpose of the Small Holes

If you look closely at an aircraft window, you may notice small holes, often referred to as "***breather holes***" or "***drain holes***." These holes serve several important functions:

Pressure Equalization: One of the primary functions of the breather holes is to allow for pressure equalization between the cabin and the space between the window layers. During flight, the cabin is pressurized to ensure passenger comfort, while the outside air pressure is significantly lower. The small holes help balance the pressure differences, reducing the risk of window failure.

Aircraft Anatomy and Systems

Preventing Moisture Accumulation: The breather holes also help prevent moisture buildup between the window layers.

If moisture were to accumulate, it could lead to fogging or icing of the windows, impairing visibility. The holes allow any moisture to drain away, maintaining a clear view for passengers and crew.

Safety: In the unlikely event of a window breach, the holes help mitigate the sudden loss of cabin pressure. By allowing for a gradual equalization, the risk of rapid decompression is reduced, contributing to overall passenger safety.

The Three Layers of an Aircraft Window

Aircraft windows typically consist of three layers, each serving a specific purpose:

Outer Layer (Polycarbonate): The outermost layer is usually made from a strong polycarbonate material that is designed to withstand impact and resist scratching. This layer protects the inner layers from external elements such as rain, hail, and debris during flight. It is also designed to handle extreme temperature variations.

Middle Layer (Acrylic): The middle layer is typically constructed from acrylic or another lightweight material. This layer provides structural support and insulation. Its primary function is to reduce the amount of noise and vibration that reaches the cabin, contributing to passenger comfort during flight.

Inner Layer (Transparent Material): The innermost layer is often made of a similar material to the outer layer, providing additional protection. This layer is directly exposed to the cabin environment and ensures passengers have a clear view outside.

The three-layer design not only enhances safety and durability but also improves comfort by maintaining cabin pressure and minimizing noise. Together, these layers work to create a secure and pleasant flying experience for all aboard.

Understanding the design and function of aircraft windows helps highlight the engineering advancements that contribute to aviation safety. The small breather holes play a vital role in pressure equalization and moisture prevention, while the three-layer construction ensures durability, insulation, and visibility. These elements are crucial for providing passengers with a safe and enjoyable journey through the skies.

The De Havilland Comet and its Square Windows

The De Havilland Comet was a pioneering aircraft in civil aviation, being the *world's first commercially successful jet airliner*. One of its distinctive features was its **square windows**, a design choice that contributed to its identity and legacy. However, the square windows posed structural challenges, being more prone to stress concentrations and fatigue, which were implicated in incidents leading to tragic accidents. These incidents prompted design changes, leading to the adoption of round windows for improved safety. Despite setbacks, the Comet remains an iconic aircraft in aviation history, with its square windows symbolizing the challenges and innovations of early jet travel.

Why plane windows are round?

Aircraft windows play a vital role in providing passengers with views of the outside world and allowing natural light to illuminate the cabin. One notable characteristic of aircraft windows is their rounded shape, as opposed to the rectangular or square windows commonly found in buildings and vehicles. In this chapter, we will explore the reasons behind the use of round aircraft windows and the advantages they offer in the context of aviation.

The sharp corners of square windows *concentrate stress*, *creating weak points* in the fuselage. This stress, compounded by the constant pressurization and depressurization cycles during flight, can lead to metal fatigue and eventual failure. Engineers realized that round windows distribute pressure more evenly along their curves, reducing the risk of stress concentration and structural failure. That's why today, airplane windows are round, to ensure your safety in the skies.

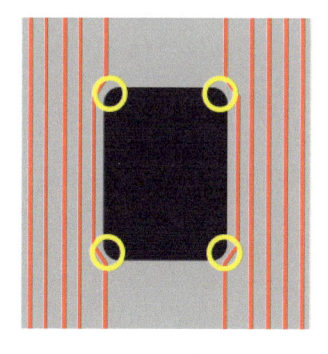

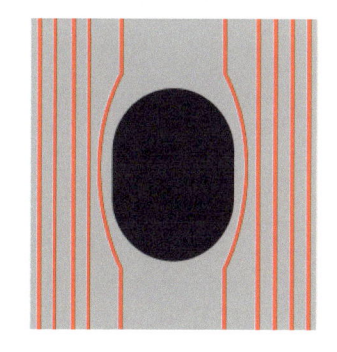

Square windows

Round windows

= Stress

Concentrate stress, creating weak points in the fuselage

Reducing the risk of stress concentration and structural failure

Aircraft Anatomy and Systems

Chapter 3

Airport Infrastructure and Operations

Runway Markings

Runway markings are an essential aspect of aviation infrastructure, providing vital visual cues to pilots during takeoff, landing, and taxiing. These markings, painted on the surface of the runway, serve as a universal language for pilots, guiding them safely through various phases of flight operations.

Understanding runway markings is crucial for pilots to maintain situational awareness and ensure the safe and efficient movement of aircraft on the ground. In this section, we will explore the different types of runway markings and their significance in aviation.

Centerline

Centerline markings run along the center of the runway and provide guidance to pilots during **takeoff**, **landing**, and **taxiing**. These markings are typically solid white lines, sometimes accompanied by dashed lines indicating the start or end of the runway.

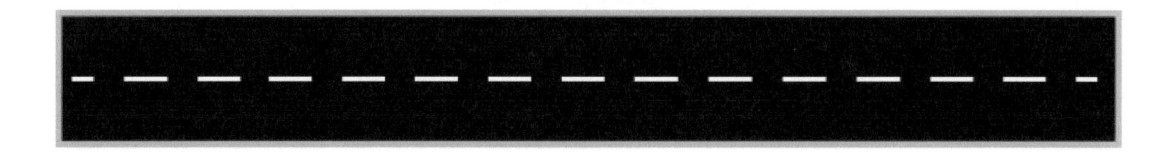

Side Stripe Markings

Side stripe markings run along the edges of the runway and serve as visual aids for pilots during taxiing. These markings are typically solid white lines, providing a clear boundary between the runway and the surrounding pavement or grass.

Aiming Point

Aiming point markings are located at the midpoint of the touchdown zone and serve as visual references for pilots during landing. They typically consist of two rectangular markings, one on each side of the centerline, indicating the desired touchdown point for landing.

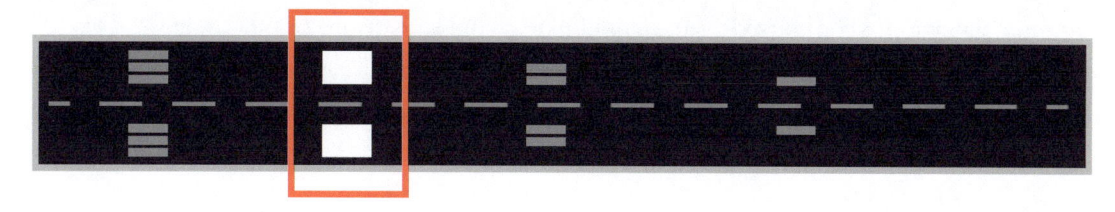

Touchdown Zone

Touchdown zone markings are located in the *first 3,000 feet* of the runway and help pilots identify the touchdown zone during landing. These markings consist of groups of white stripes perpendicular to the centerline, *with each group spanning 500 feet*.

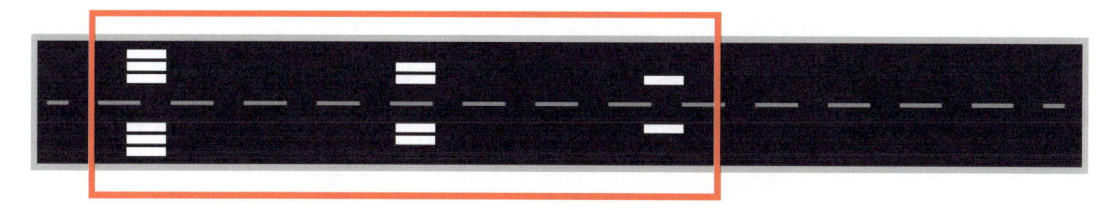

Threshold Markings

Threshold markings are located at each end of the runway and indicate the beginning of the available landing distance. These markings consist of thick white lines perpendicular to the runway centerline, extending across the full width of the runway. They serve as a visual reference for pilots, helping them identify the threshold of the runway during approach and landing maneuvers.

Airport Infrastructure and Operations

Runway Digits

Runway designation numbers, commonly known as runway digits, play a crucial role in the identification and orientation of runways at airports worldwide. These numerical markings are not arbitrarily placed but follow an international standard aimed at providing pilots with clear and precise information regarding the orientation of runways. Here are the main reasons for the presence of specific numbers on runways:

Magnetic Alignment

The numbers on a runway represent the magnetic alignment of the runway in degrees. This means that the numbers indicate the direction in which the runway is aligned, based on the magnetic north pole. For example, the number "**09**" represents a runway aligned in the direction of *90 degrees*, i.e., east.

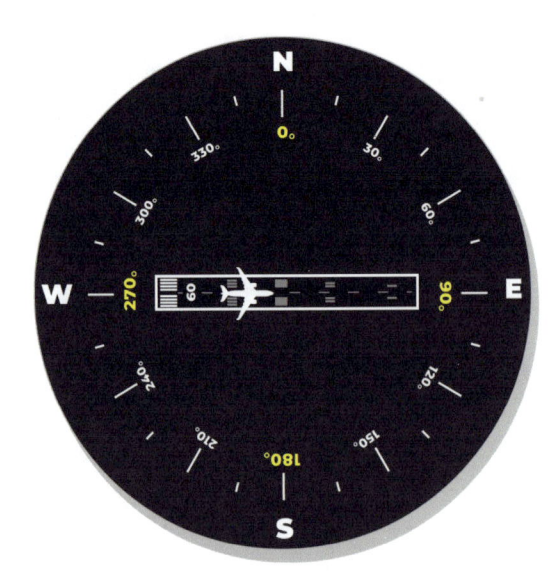

Essential Taxiway Markings and Signs

Taxiway markings and signs are essential components of airport surface navigation, guiding pilots safely from the gate to the runway and back. These visual aids ensure that aircraft operate in the correct areas and avoid conflicts with other aircraft or ground vehicles. In this chapter, we'll cover key taxiway markings and signs, explaining what each one means and its significance in safe ground operations.

Non-Movement Area Marking

Non-movement area markings define the boundary between the movement and non-movement areas of an airport. Movement areas are those where pilots must communicate with Air Traffic Control (**ATC**) for clearance to move, such as taxiways and runways. Non-movement areas are typically apron or ramp areas where aircraft are parked, refueled, or loaded, and where ATC clearance is not required for movement.

- Marking Description: A non-movement area is marked by two yellow lines a solid line and a dashed line. The solid line is on the non-movement side, and the dashed line is on the movement area side.

- Purpose: Pilots must stop and obtain clearance before crossing from the non-movement area into the movement area. No clearance is needed to taxi within the non-movement area.

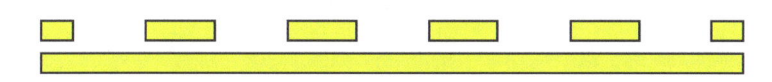

ATC MOVEMENT AREA
(UNDER ATC CONTROL)

ATC NON-MOVEMENT AREA
(NOT UNDER ATC CONTROL)

Taxiway Direction Signs

Taxiway direction signs provide pilots with guidance on which taxiways lead to certain destinations, such as runways, gates, or other taxiways. These signs are typically found at intersections of taxiways.

Appearance: Direction signs are black letters and numbers on a yellow background with an arrow pointing in the direction of the specified taxiway. For example, "D →" means Taxiway Delta is to the right.

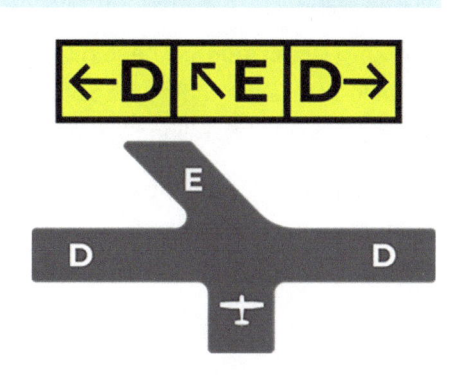

Purpose: These signs help pilots navigate the airport surface and ensure they take the correct path to their intended destination. They are especially useful in large airports with complex taxiway networks.

Airport Infrastructure and Operations | 61

Taxiway Location Signs

Taxiway location signs indicate the current taxiway the aircraft is on. These are critical for pilots to maintain situational awareness during taxi operations.

Appearance: Location signs have yellow letters or numbers on a black background with a yellow border. For example, "E" indicates Taxiway Echo.

Purpose: These signs confirm the aircraft's current position on the taxiway system, helping pilots avoid getting lost or entering the wrong taxiway.

Taxi Holding Position Markings

Taxi holding position markings are found on taxiways and indicate the location where an aircraft must stop and hold until it receives further clearance from ATC, typically before crossing a runway or entering an active taxiway.

Marking Description: These markings consist of four yellow lines, two solid and two dashed, running across the width of the taxiway. The solid lines are on the side where the aircraft must stop, and the dashed lines are on the side facing the runway.

Purpose: These markings ensure that aircraft do not enter a runway or critical area without clearance, preventing conflicts with landing or departing aircraft.

HOLD SHORT OF INTERSECTING TAXIWAY WHEN DIRECTED BY ATC

Airport Infrastructure and Operations

Runway Holding Position Markings

Runway holding position markings are placed at the intersection of a taxiway and a runway, indicating where an aircraft must stop before entering the runway.

Marking Description: These markings are similar to taxi holding position markings, consisting of four yellow lines—two solid and two dashed. They are located across the taxiway before the runway threshold.

Purpose: Pilots must stop at this marking and await clearance from ATC before crossing or entering the runway. This is a critical safety measure to prevent runway incursions.

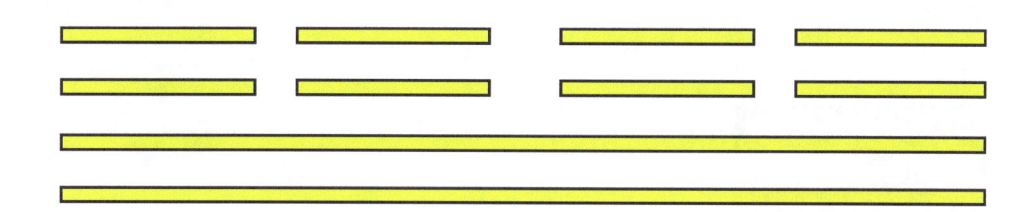

Enhanced Taxiway Centerline Markings

Enhanced taxiway centerline markings are designed to give pilots additional awareness as they approach runway holding positions. These markings are typically used at larger airports where high traffic or complex taxiway systems exist.

Marking Description: Enhanced centerlines are yellow dashed lines parallel to the standard solid yellow taxiway centerline. They are usually spaced about 3 feet apart and extend 150 feet before the runway holding position.

Purpose: The enhanced centerline serves as a visual cue to remind pilots that they are nearing a runway holding position and must be prepared to stop.

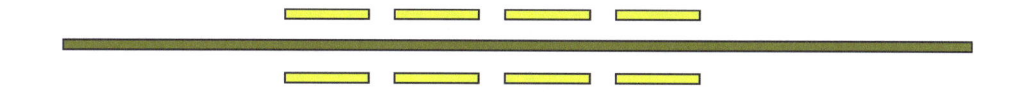

Airport Infrastructure and Operations

Runway Position Signs

Runway position signs indicate that an aircraft is about to enter a runway and must not proceed without clearance. These signs are crucial for preventing runway incursions, especially at busy airports.

Appearance: Runway position signs have white numbers on a red background. For example, **"25L-7R"** means the aircraft is approaching the intersection of Runway 25L and Runway 7R.

Purpose: These signs alert pilots that they are at a runway threshold and must wait for ATC clearance before proceeding onto the runway.

ILS Critical Area Markings

The Instrument Landing System (**ILS**) critical area is a sensitive area near a runway where interference from aircraft or vehicles can disrupt the precision signals used by incoming aircraft during instrument approaches.

Marking Description: ILS critical area markings are similar to taxi holding position markings but have an additional vertical yellow line across the center. These markings are placed on taxiways near runways equipped with an ILS system.

Purpose: When low-visibility conditions are present, aircraft must stop at this line to avoid interfering with ILS signals. ATC typically advises pilots when to hold short of this area.

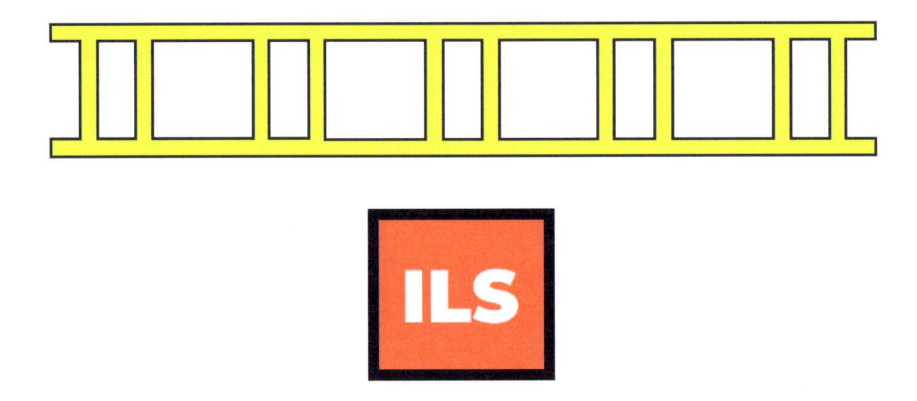

Airport Infrastructure and Operations

Taxiway markings and signs play an integral role in the safety and efficiency of airport ground operations. From non-movement area markings to runway holding position signs, each element provides critical information to pilots, helping them navigate the airport surface safely and avoid potentially hazardous situations. Understanding and correctly interpreting these visual aids is essential for every pilot, ensuring smooth ground operations and preventing runway incursions.

How Windsocks Work

Windsocks, also known as wind cones, are simple yet essential tools in aviation, providing quick visual information about wind direction and strength. Found at airports, helipads, and even smaller airstrips, they play a crucial role in ensuring safe takeoffs and landings. Let's explore how they work and why they're so important.

Structure of a Windsock

A windsock consists of two main parts:

The Frame: This is typically a metal ring or rigid structure at the mouth of the windsock, attached to a pole. The frame allows the windsock to rotate freely based on the wind direction.

The Fabric Sock: The sock is usually made from a durable, weather-resistant fabric. It tapers from the wider opening at the frame down to a narrow, closed end. Its conical shape helps it catch the wind efficiently.

How Windsocks Indicate Wind Direction

Windsocks are designed to point in the direction from which the wind is blowing. When the wind blows into the open end of the sock, it causes the fabric to lift and point toward the opposite direction. For example, if the wind is coming from the north, the windsock will point south. This allows pilots to quickly understand the wind direction by looking at the orientation of the windsock.

How Windsocks Measure Wind Speed

While windsocks are primarily used to indicate wind direction, they can also provide a rough estimate of wind speed. This is where the alternating colored bands—typically orange and white—come into play. Many windsocks are designed with several bands, and the number of bands that inflate gives a visual cue to the wind speed.

Here's a more detailed breakdown of how to interpret wind speed using a windsock:

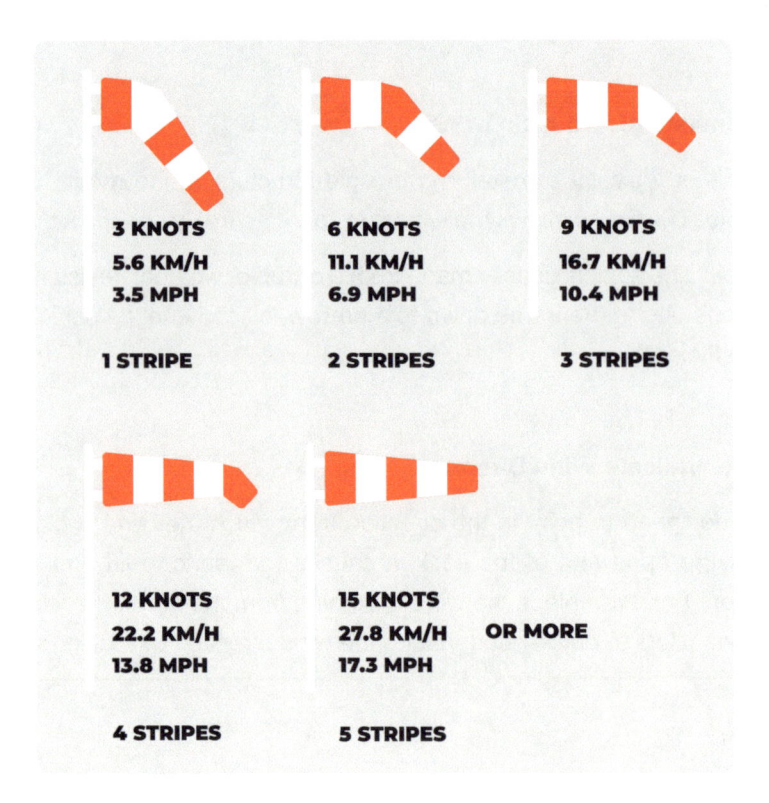

3 KNOTS 5.6 KM/H 3.5 MPH 1 STRIPE	6 KNOTS 11.1 KM/H 6.9 MPH 2 STRIPES	9 KNOTS 16.7 KM/H 10.4 MPH 3 STRIPES
12 KNOTS 22.2 KM/H 13.8 MPH 4 STRIPES	15 KNOTS 27.8 KM/H OR MORE 17.3 MPH 5 STRIPES	

Airport Infrastructure and Operations

The Importance of Windsocks in Aviation

In aviation, wind direction and speed are critical factors in determining the safest runway for takeoff and landing. Aircraft perform best when taking off and landing into a headwind, as it provides more lift and reduces the distance required for the aircraft to become airborne or come to a stop. Conversely, tailwinds can increase the required runway length and make landing more difficult, especially for smaller aircraft.

Crosswinds—winds blowing perpendicular to the runway—can be particularly challenging. Windsocks help pilots visually assess whether crosswinds are manageable for their aircraft, or if an alternative runway or approach should be used.

Windsock Standards and Regulations

Windsocks used in aviation must adhere to certain standards to ensure they are reliable under various conditions. In many countries, the dimensions and visibility requirements are regulated:

Length: Windsocks are typically between 8 and 12 feet (**2.4 to 3.7 meters**) long, with the wide opening being around 18 inches (**45 centimeters**) in diameter.

Color: The alternating color bands (**often orange and white**) are designed for high visibility during both day and night. Many windsocks are also equipped with lighting or reflective material for use at night or in low visibility conditions.

In addition, some airports have more than one windsock to account for varying wind conditions in different parts of the airfield. Large airports may have illuminated windsocks at multiple points along the runways to provide comprehensive wind information.

PAPI Lights

Navigating an aircraft safely during approach and landing is critical for pilots, especially in low visibility conditions or at night. Precision Approach Path Indicator (**PAPI**) lights are a crucial visual aid that helps pilots maintain the correct glide path for a safe landing. In this chapter, we will delve into the function, configuration, and significance of PAPI lights in aviation.

Function of PAPI Lights:

Guiding the Glide Path

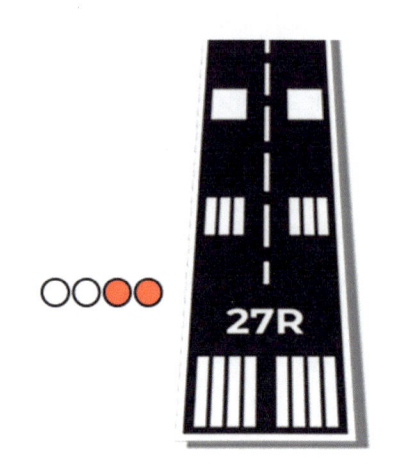

PAPI lights are installed alongside the runway and are typically located on the left-hand side. They emit a combination of red and white lights that provide visual cues to pilots regarding their aircraft's vertical position relative to the ideal glide path for landing.

Visual Reference for Pilots:

By observing the color combination of the PAPI lights, pilots can determine if their aircraft is above, below, or on the correct glide path. A combination of two white lights indicates that the aircraft is above the glide path, while a combination of two red lights indicates that the aircraft is below the glide path. An equal number of red and white lights indicates that the aircraft is on the correct glide path.

CORRECT APPROACH

TOO HIGH

TOO LOW

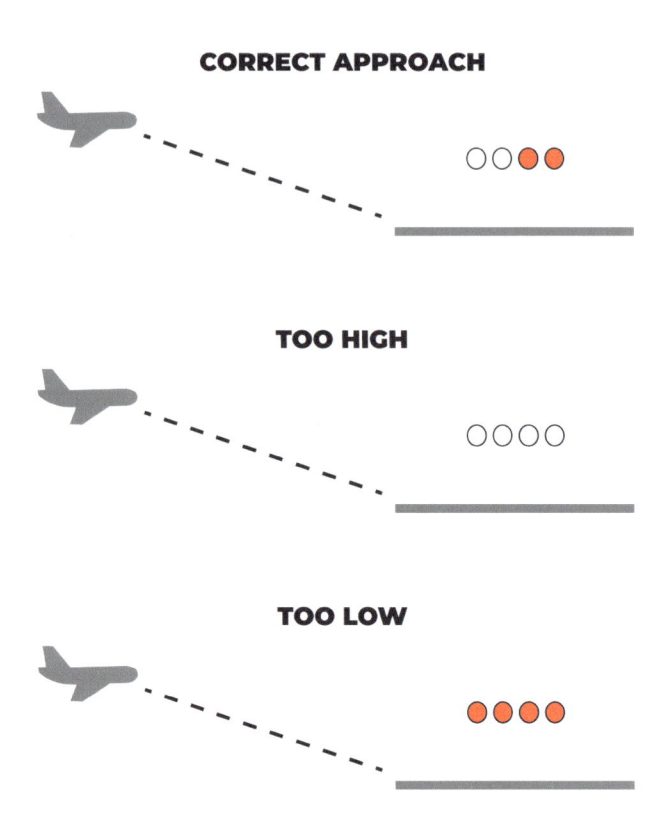

Configuration of PAPI Lights:

Four-Light Configuration:

The most common configuration of PAPI lights consists of four lights arranged in a row. These lights are typically mounted on a single support structure and are spaced evenly apart along the runway. Pilots can interpret the color combination of these lights to adjust their aircraft's vertical position during approach.

Significance of PAPI Lights:

Enhanced Situational Awareness:

PAPI lights provide pilots with an additional visual reference during the critical phase of approach and landing. By maintaining the correct glide path indicated by the PAPI lights, pilots can ensure a smooth and safe touchdown on the runway.

Improved Safety and Precision:

PAPI lights contribute to enhanced safety and precision during landing operations, particularly in adverse weather conditions or at airports with challenging terrain. They enable pilots to make real-time adjustments to their descent rate, reducing the risk of undershooting or overshooting the runway.

Precision Approach Path Indicator (**PAPI**) lights are indispensable tools that aid pilots in maintaining the correct glide path during approach and landing. By providing clear visual cues, PAPI lights enhance situational awareness and contribute to safer and more precise landings, ultimately ensuring the smooth operation of air traffic at airports worldwide.

Understanding Airport Codes

What Are Airport Codes?

Airport codes are unique identifiers assigned to airports worldwide. These codes are essential for air travel, helping pilots, air traffic controllers, and passengers identify airports quickly and without confusion. There are three primary systems of airport codes:

IATA Codes (International Air Transport Association)

ICAO Codes (International Civil Aviation Organization)

FAA Codes (Federal Aviation Administration, used in the United States)

Each system serves a specific purpose and has unique characteristics.

IATA Codes

What Are IATA Codes?

IATA codes are three-letter codes used in airline timetables, tickets, and baggage tags. These codes are designed for convenience and are familiar to the general public.

How Are IATA Codes Created?

IATA codes often reflect the airport's name, location, or historical significance. For example:

- **LAX:** Los Angeles International Airport
- **JFK:** John F. Kennedy International Airport in New York
- **DXB:** Dubai International Airport

Characteristics

User-Friendly: IATA codes are easy to remember and are used by passengers, airlines, and travel agencies.

Regional Variations: Some codes are derived from local names or languages.

Limitations: Since there are only 17,576 possible combinations (**26 letters, three places**), some codes may appear similar or unrelated to their location.

ICAO Codes

What Are ICAO Codes?

ICAO codes are four-letter codes used for flight operations, air traffic control, and navigation. Unlike IATA codes, they are less familiar to the general public but provide more detailed information about the airport's location.

How Are ICAO Codes Created?

ICAO codes follow a regional prefix system:

The First Letter: Indicates the region.

The Second Letter: Indicates the country.

The Remaining Letters: Identify the specific airport.

For example:

- **KJFK:** John F. Kennedy International Airport (**"K" indicates the United States**).
- **EGLL:** London Heathrow Airport (**"EG" is for the United Kingdom**).
- **RJAA:** Narita International Airport, Tokyo (**"RJ" is for Japan**).

Characteristics

Global Standard: ICAO codes are recognized worldwide and provide exact location details.

Operational Use: These codes are used for filing flight plans, air traffic communication, and airport databases.

More Combinations: With four letters, ICAO codes can accommodate many more airports.

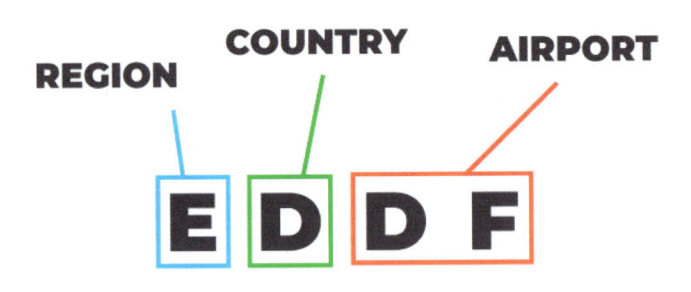

```
REGION   COUNTRY   AIRPORT
   E        D        D F
```

EDDF = Frankfurt, Germany

FAA Codes - or FAA LIDs (FAA Location Identifiers)

What Are FAA Codes?

FAA codes are three-letter codes used only within the United States. In many cases, they are the same as IATA codes, but there are exceptions for smaller or less commercially used airports.

How Are FAA Codes Created?

The FAA assigns these codes to airports not covered by IATA. They may appear similar but are distinct from IATA and ICAO systems.

For Example:

- **IATA/FAA Match:** ATL (**Hartsfield-Jackson Atlanta International Airport**).
- **FAA Only:** IATA does not assign codes to some general aviation airports, but the FAA does, such as SNA for John Wayne Airport in California.

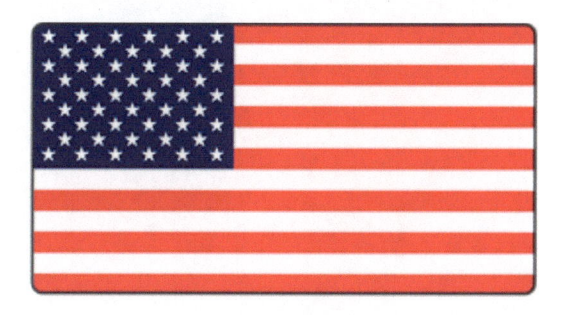

Why Do We Need Three Systems?

Each code system has its specific purpose:

IATA Codes: Passenger convenience and airline operations.

ICAO Codes: International aviation operations and air traffic control.

FAA Codes: Domestic use within the United States for smaller or non-commercial airports.

Having multiple systems ensures flexibility and precision for both operational and public-facing needs.

Chapter 4

Flight Instruments and Avionics

6 PACK Aircraft Instruments

Aircraft instruments are essential for pilots to safely and efficiently operate an airplane. These instruments provide critical information about the aircraft's performance, navigation, and environment. This chapter delves into the primary types of aircraft instruments, elaborating on their functions and importance in aviation.

Airspeed Indicator

The airspeed indicator measures the aircraft's speed relative to the surrounding air, typically displayed in knots. Knowing the airspeed is essential for various phases of flight, such as takeoff, cruising, and landing. Maintaining appropriate speeds is crucial to prevent stalling or overspeed conditions, ensuring the aircraft operates within its safe performance envelope.

Altimeter

The altimeter measures the aircraft's altitude above sea level. The altimeter works by comparing the atmospheric pressure outside the aircraft to a standard pressure value, typically adjusted for local conditions using the QNH setting. This information is critical for ensuring the aircraft maintains safe separation from the ground and other obstacles, especially during approaches and landings. Accurate altitude readings are also necessary for complying with air traffic control instructions and maintaining prescribed flight levels.

Flight Instruments and Avionics

Attitude Indicator

The attitude indicator, also known as the artificial horizon, displays the aircraft's orientation relative to the horizon. This instrument shows the pitch (**nose up or down**) and bank (**left or right tilt**) of the aircraft. It is particularly useful in conditions of poor visibility, such as in clouds or at night, where the natural horizon is not visible. By maintaining the correct pitch and bank angles, pilots can ensure the aircraft remains stable and on the intended flight path, avoiding dangerous attitudes that could lead to loss of control.

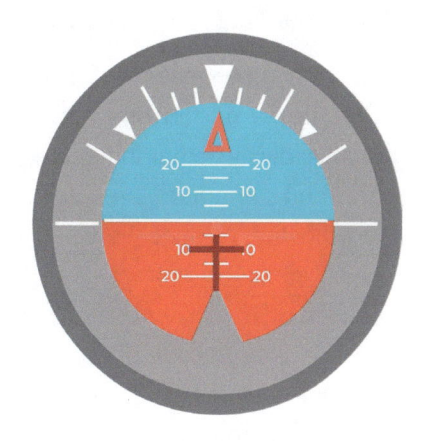

Heading Indicator

The heading indicator shows the aircraft's direction relative to magnetic north. Unlike the magnetic compass, which can be affected by acceleration and turning errors, the heading indicator provides a stable reference for navigation. Pilots regularly cross-check the heading indicator with the magnetic compass and adjust for any discrepancies. This instrument is essential for maintaining accurate navigation along planned routes and during instrument approaches.

Vertical Speed Indicator

The vertical speed indicator (**VSI**) measures the rate of climb or descent in feet per minute. The VSI helps pilots maintain controlled climbs and descents, avoiding abrupt altitude changes that could be uncomfortable for passengers or lead to potential conflicts with other air traffic. By monitoring the vertical speed, pilots can make smooth transitions between different flight levels and ensure compliance with air traffic control clearances.

Flight Instruments and Avionics

Turn Coordinator

The turn coordinator is an instrument that indicates the rate of turn and the quality of the turn. It shows whether the aircraft is turning left or right and whether the turn is coordinated, meaning the balance between the aileron and rudder inputs is correct. The turn coordinator consists of a miniature airplane silhouette that banks in the direction of the turn and a ball in a tube that indicates the quality of the turn. If the ball is centered, the turn is coordinated; if not, the aircraft is either skidding or slipping. This instrument is particularly useful in instrument flight conditions where visual references to the horizon are not available.

These six instruments—airspeed indicator, altimeter, attitude indicator, heading indicator, vertical speed indicator, and turn coordinator—are collectively known as the "**six pack**" and are fundamental for safe and effective aircraft operation. By mastering the use of these instruments, pilots can navigate the skies with confidence and ensure the safety of everyone on board.

Avionics - The Brain of the Aircraft

Avionics refers to the electronic systems used on aircraft, encompassing a wide range of functions that are crucial for navigation, communication, monitoring, and control. These systems have evolved dramatically over the years, transitioning from mechanical devices to sophisticated digital technologies that enhance safety and efficiency in modern aviation. Understanding avionics is essential for pilots, engineers, and aviation enthusiasts alike.

Components of Avionics

Global Positioning System (GPS): GPS is a satellite-based navigation system that provides accurate position information. It allows pilots to determine their location in real-time and is integral to modern navigation.

Inertial Navigation System (INS): INS uses a combination of gyroscopes and accelerometers to calculate an aircraft's position and orientation without external references. This system is often used in conjunction with GPS for redundancy and accuracy.

Communication Systems

VHF Radio: Very High Frequency (**VHF**) radios are the primary means of communication between pilots and air traffic control (**ATC**). They operate within the VHF band and allow for voice communication over various frequencies.

Data Link Communications: Systems such as ACARS (**Aircraft Communications Addressing and Reporting System**) enable text-based communication between the aircraft and ground services, allowing for the transmission of flight information, weather updates, and maintenance reports.

Flight Instrumentation

Primary Flight Display (PFD): The PFD consolidates critical flight information, including altitude, airspeed, attitude, and navigation data, onto a single screen, providing pilots with a comprehensive overview of the aircraft's status.

Multi-Function Display (MFD): MFDs present a variety of information, such as weather data, terrain awareness, and navigation charts, allowing pilots to access multiple data sources at once.

Autopilot Systems

Basic Autopilot: This system can control the aircraft's heading and altitude, relieving pilots of some routine flying tasks.

Advanced Autopilot (FMS): The Flight Management System (**FMS**) integrates with GPS and other systems to manage the flight path, optimize fuel consumption, and automate navigation, allowing for greater efficiency and precision during flight.

Weather Radar and Monitoring

Doppler Radar: Weather radar systems help pilots detect and navigate around severe weather conditions, such as thunderstorms, by providing real-time information about precipitation and turbulence.

Turbulence Detection Systems: These systems use sensors to identify and alert pilots to areas of potential turbulence, improving passenger comfort and safety.

Benefits of Modern Avionics

The integration of advanced avionics systems into aircraft has led to numerous benefits, including:

Enhanced Safety: Improved situational awareness through real-time data and alerts helps pilots make informed decisions, reducing the likelihood of accidents.

Increased Efficiency: Automation and optimized flight paths lead to better fuel management and reduced operational costs.

Greater Precision: Digital technologies enable more accurate navigation and control, particularly during challenging flight conditions such as low visibility.

Challenges and Considerations

Despite the advantages, modern avionics also present challenges:

- Complexity: The increasing sophistication of avionics systems requires pilots to undergo extensive training and maintain a deep understanding of their operation.

- Reliability and Redundancy: Ensuring that avionics systems function correctly is critical, necessitating redundancy and regular maintenance to mitigate the risk of system failures.

Avionics are an essential component of modern aircraft, serving as the brain that facilitates communication, navigation, and control. As technology continues to evolve, avionics systems will undoubtedly become even more advanced, further enhancing the safety and efficiency of aviation. Understanding these systems is crucial for anyone involved in the aviation industry, from pilots to engineers, as they play a pivotal role in the overall success of flight operations.

Flight Envelope Protection Systems

Modern aircraft are equipped with advanced technologies to enhance flight safety, and one of the most critical innovations is Flight Envelope Protection. These systems prevent pilots from inadvertently exceeding the aircraft's operational limits, thereby protecting both the aircraft and its occupants from dangerous situations. Flight envelope protection is especially valuable in preventing incidents caused by human error, adverse weather conditions, or mechanical failures.

What is the Flight Envelope?

The flight envelope refers to the boundaries within which an aircraft can safely operate. These boundaries are defined by various factors, including:

- **Airspeed:** The aircraft must maintain a minimum and maximum safe speed.
- **Altitude:** Structural limits exist for how high or low an aircraft can safely fly.
- **G-forces:** Limits on how much acceleration (positive or negative) the aircraft can withstand without structural damage.
- **Angle of Attack (AoA):** The angle between the aircraft's wings and the oncoming airflow. Too high an angle can lead to a stall.

Operating outside these boundaries can result in loss of control, structural failure, or other dangerous conditions. Flight envelope protection systems are designed to ensure that the aircraft remains within these safe parameters, even in challenging situations.

How Flight Envelope Protection Works

Most modern commercial aircraft, especially those with fly-by-wire systems, are equipped with flight envelope protection. Fly-by-wire replaces traditional mechanical flight controls with an electronic interface, allowing the aircraft's computers to assist in managing flight parameters. These computers continuously monitor flight conditions and intervene if the aircraft is at risk of exceeding its safe limits.

Some of the key functions of flight envelope protection include:

Stall Protection

Stall occurs when the aircraft's angle of attack becomes too high, causing a loss of lift. Envelope protection prevents this by limiting the maximum angle of attack the aircraft can reach. If a pilot pulls back too aggressively on the control stick, the system will prevent the nose from raising beyond a safe angle.

Overspeed Protection

Overspeed protection prevents the aircraft from flying too fast, which could lead to structural damage or control difficulties. If the aircraft approaches its maximum safe speed (known as Vmo/Mmo), the system will automatically reduce the engine power or adjust the pitch to slow the aircraft down.

G-Load Protection

To protect the structural integrity of the aircraft, G-load protection ensures that the forces exerted on the aircraft remain within the safe limits. For example, during aggressive maneuvers, the system limits how much positive or negative G-force the aircraft can endure.

Bank Angle Protection

Aircraft have a maximum safe bank angle (the degree to which the aircraft can roll sideways). Exceeding this angle could cause loss of control. Envelope protection systems limit the maximum bank angle, ensuring the aircraft remains stable during turns and maneuvers.

Pitch Protection

Pitch protection prevents the aircraft from excessively pitching up or down. This feature is especially useful during takeoff or landing when rapid pitch changes could lead to a stall or overspeed.

Load Factor Protection

Load factor protection ensures that the vertical forces acting on the aircraft (both positive and negative) are kept within safe limits, preventing overloading of the aircraft structure during high-speed or high-angle maneuvers.

Examples of Flight Envelope Protection Systems

Flight envelope protection is common in modern fly-by-wire aircraft such as the Airbus A320, A350, Boeing 787, and other advanced commercial aircraft. Here are a few key examples of these systems in action:

Airbus

Airbus aircraft are equipped with fly-by-wire systems that provide multiple layers of protection. The Airbus flight control system includes a Normal Law, which ensures the aircraft remains within the flight envelope. If the system detects that the aircraft is approaching its limits, it will automatically override pilot inputs to prevent an unsafe situation.

In Normal Law, the Airbus flight control system provides:

- **Pitch protection:** Limits pitch-up and pitch-down angles.
- **Bank angle protection:** Limits roll angles to prevent excessive banking.
- **Stall protection:** Prevents the aircraft from exceeding the critical angle of attack.
- **Overspeed protection:** Limits speed to prevent structural damage.

If an abnormal situation occurs, the system can degrade to Alternate Law or Direct Law, where some protections are reduced or removed, but the aircraft still maintains basic handling characteristics.

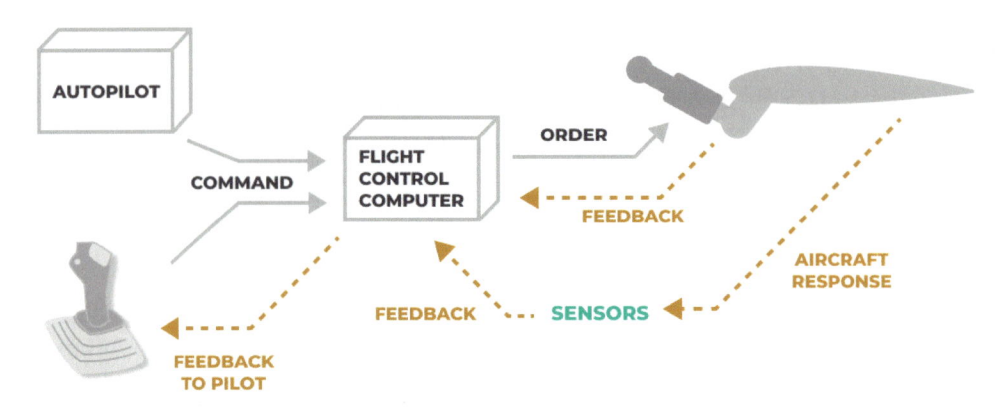

Fly By Wire System

Boeing

Boeing's approach to flight envelope protection is slightly different. While Boeing aircraft such as the 787 Dreamliner use fly-by-wire technology, the design philosophy allows pilots more direct control of the aircraft. Boeing systems provide soft limits, meaning the pilot can override certain protections in critical situations. For instance, the aircraft will alert the pilot if it is nearing stall or overspeed, but the system does not automatically prevent the aircraft from exceeding these limits.

Benefits of Flight Envelope Protection

The advantages of flight envelope protection are numerous:

Increased Safety: By preventing pilots from unintentionally exceeding the aircraft's operational limits, flight envelope protection reduces the risk of accidents due to pilot error.

Reduced Pilot Workload: Automation and protection systems relieve pilots of the need to constantly monitor and adjust flight parameters, allowing them to focus on higher-level decision-making.

Improved Aircraft Performance: Pilots can confidently fly the aircraft closer to its maximum performance limits, knowing that the system will intervene if necessary.

Limitations and Challenges

While flight envelope protection offers many benefits, it is not without its limitations:

- **Over-reliance on Automation:** Pilots may become too dependent on the systems, leading to skill degradation or slow reactions in cases where manual control is required.

- **Failure Scenarios**: While these systems are designed with redundancy, they are still subject to failures, and pilots must be trained to handle situations where envelope protection may not be available.

- **System Degradation:** In certain abnormal flight conditions, such as multiple system failures, the flight envelope protection may degrade or become unavailable, requiring the pilot to rely more heavily on manual controls.

The Black Box

In the realm of aviation, the "*Black Box*" is one of the most critical components for ensuring flight safety and for investigating incidents and accidents. Despite its name, the Black Box is not black; it is typically bright orange to make it easier to locate after an accident. This chapter delves into what the Black Box is, its components, and its importance in aviation.

What is the Black Box?

The term "*Black Box*" refers to two crucial flight recording devices found on aircraft:

- **Flight Data Recorder (FDR)**
- **Cockpit Voice Recorder (CVR)**

These devices are designed to withstand extreme conditions and to provide investigators with essential data in the event of an incident or accident.

Cockpit Voice Recorder

Flight Data Recorder

Flight Data Recorder (FDR)

- **Function:** The FDR records various operational parameters of the aircraft.

- **Data Recorded:** Parameters such as airspeed, altitude, vertical acceleration, heading, engine performance, and control surface positions.

- **Duration:** Typically records at least 25 hours of flight data, continuously overwriting the oldest data to ensure the most recent information is available.

The FDR provides a comprehensive picture of the aircraft's performance and operational state leading up to an incident. This data is crucial for investigators to understand what happened during a flight and to identify any mechanical or systemic issues.

Cockpit Voice Recorder (CVR)

- **Function:** The CVR captures audio recordings from the cockpit, including conversations between the flight crew, ambient cockpit sounds, and communications with air traffic control (**ATC**).

- **Data Recorded:** Microphone inputs from headsets, cockpit area microphone (**CAM**) for capturing ambient sounds, and radio transmissions.

- **Duration:** Typically records the last 2 hours of audio, continuously overwriting older recordings.

The CVR is vital for understanding the human factors and decision-making processes in the cockpit. It helps investigators determine what the crew was discussing and doing in the moments leading up to an incident, providing insights into potential human errors, communication breakdowns, or other cockpit dynamics.

Construction and Durability

Design

Both the FDR and CVR are built to endure extreme conditions that might be encountered in an accident:

- **Crashworthiness:** Constructed to survive high-impact forces.
- **Fire Resistance:** Able to withstand temperatures up to 1,100°C (**2,012°F**) for at least 30 minutes.
- **Waterproofing:** Designed to be waterproof and to survive underwater for extended periods.

Location Devices

Underwater Locator Beacon (ULB): Attached to both the FDR and CVR, the ULB emits ultrasonic pulses when submerged in water, aiding search teams in locating the devices.

The Black Box is an indispensable tool in aviation, providing essential data that helps ensure the safety and reliability of air travel. Through rigorous analysis of the information captured by the FDR and CVR, the aviation industry can continuously learn from incidents and implement measures to enhance flight safety. Understanding the role and functionality of the Black Box underscores its importance in maintaining the high standards of modern aviation.

GPS in Aviation

Global Positioning System (**GPS**) technology has revolutionized aviation by providing precise and reliable navigation information. This chapter covers the basics of GPS, its benefits, and its applications in aviation.

Introduction to GPS

GPS is a satellite-based navigation system that provides location and time information anywhere on Earth. It consists of a constellation of at least 24 satellites orbiting the Earth, ground control stations, and GPS receivers.

How GPS Works

Satellites: GPS satellites transmit signals containing the satellite's location and the exact time the signal was sent.

Receivers: A GPS receiver on an aircraft picks up signals from multiple satellites and calculates its position based on the time delay of the received signals.

Triangulation: By using signals from at least four satellites, the receiver triangulates its precise location (**latitude, longitude, and altitude**).

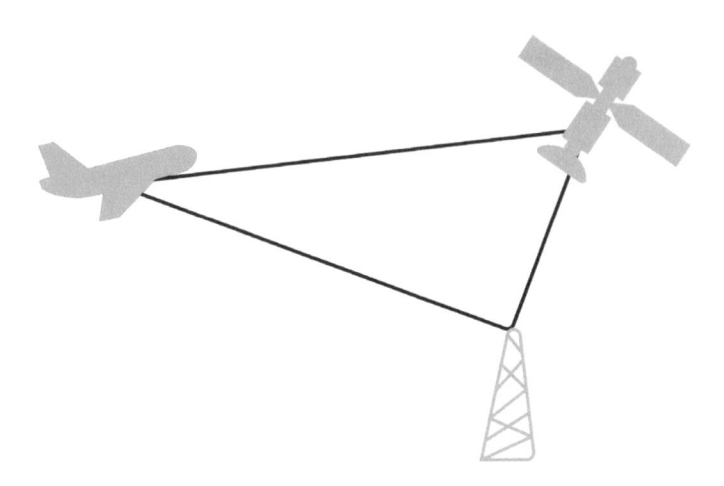

Benefits of GPS in Aviation

Accuracy: GPS provides highly accurate position information, improving navigation precision.

Coverage: GPS is available globally, enabling navigation in remote areas where traditional navigation aids may be unavailable.

Efficiency: GPS enhances flight efficiency by enabling direct routing, reducing fuel consumption and flight time.

Safety: Provides reliable information for situational awareness, aiding in collision avoidance and emergency navigation.

Applications of GPS in Aviation

Navigation: Primary means of navigation for en-route, terminal, and approach phases of flight.

Instrument Approaches: Enables precision approaches (**e.g., GPS or RNAV approaches**) to airports without ground-based navigation aids.

Situational Awareness: Enhances pilot situational awareness with moving maps and real-time position information.

Search and Rescue: Assists in locating downed aircraft and improving response times in emergencies.

Practical Tips for Using GPS

Pre-flight Checks: Ensure the GPS receiver is functioning correctly and updated with the latest database.

Cross-Check: Always cross-check GPS information with other navigation sources and instruments.

Waypoints: Use waypoints effectively to plan and execute flight routes accurately.

RAIM Checks: Perform Receiver Autonomous Integrity Monitoring (**RAIM**) checks to ensure GPS signal integrity.

Aircraft Transponders

Transponders are vital components in modern aviation, playing a crucial role in aircraft identification, communication with air traffic control (**ATC**), and enhancing overall flight safety. This chapter explores the functions of transponders, the different types available, and the key transponder codes that every pilot should know.

Introduction to Transponders

A transponder (**short for transmitter-responder**) is an electronic device that automatically responds to interrogation signals from ground-based radar systems. By sending back a signal with the aircraft's unique code and other information, transponders help ATC track and identify aircraft more accurately and efficiently.

TRANSPONDER = TRANSMITS RESPONDS

Functions of Transponders

Transponders perform several essential functions:

- **Identification:** Transponders transmit a unique identifier (**Squawk code**) assigned by ATC, helping controllers distinguish between multiple aircraft on their radar screens.

- **Altitude Reporting:** Mode C and Mode S transponders report the aircraft's altitude, providing vertical positioning data to ATC.

- **Collision Avoidance:** Mode S transponders are part of the Traffic Collision Avoidance System (**TCAS**), which alerts pilots to potential mid-air collision threats.

- **Enhanced Surveillance:** Mode S transponders can transmit additional data, such as flight number, speed, and heading.

Types of Transponders

There are several types of transponders, each with different capabilities:

- **Mode A:** Provides a four-digit identification code but does not report altitude.
- **Mode C:** Provides both identification and altitude information.
- **Mode S:** Provides identification, altitude, and additional data for enhanced surveillance and TCAS compatibility.

Key Transponder Codes

Pilots use specific transponder codes, known as Squawk codes, to communicate different situations to ATC. Here are some of the most important codes:

- **1200:** VFR (**Visual Flight Rules**) operations in the United States. This is the default code for aircraft flying under VFR conditions.
- **7000:** VFR operations in Europe. Similar to 1200 in the U.S., this is the standard VFR code for European airspace.
- **7500:** Hijacking. This code alerts ATC to a hijacking situation. It is rarely used but critical for emergency communication.
- **7600:** Radio communication failure. This code indicates that the aircraft has lost radio contact with ATC.
- **7700:** General emergency. This code is used for any other emergency situations requiring immediate attention from ATC.

Operation and Use of Transponders

Setting the Code:

- Pilots set the transponder code using a control panel, typically found in the cockpit.
- The assigned Squawk code is provided by ATC before departure or during flight.

Mode Selection:

- Ensure the transponder is set to the appropriate mode (**A, C, or S**) based on the flight requirements.
- Mode C or S should be used when altitude reporting is required.

Ident Feature:

- The "Ident" button temporarily highlights the aircraft on ATC radar, making it easier for controllers to identify it.
- Use this feature when requested by ATC.

Best Practices and Maintenance

Regular Testing:

- Perform regular transponder tests and checks to ensure proper functionality.
- Ground checks can verify the accuracy of code transmission and altitude reporting.

Compliance with Regulations:

- Always follow ATC instructions regarding transponder use and code settings.
- Be aware of regional differences in standard VFR codes (**e.g., 1200 in the U.S., 7000 in Europe**).

Responding to Alerts:

- If ATC advises of an incorrect transponder code or malfunction, rectify the issue promptly.
- In the event of a code-related emergency (**e.g., 7500, 7600, 7700**), follow established emergency procedures.

QNH, QFE & QNE

Altimeters are crucial instruments in an aircraft, helping pilots determine their altitude above sea level. Correct altimeter settings are essential for safe flight operations, ensuring accurate altitude readings and maintaining safe separation from the ground and other aircraft. This chapter explains what altimeter settings are, why they are important, and how to use them.

What is an Altimeter?

An altimeter is an instrument that measures the altitude of an aircraft. It works by measuring the atmospheric pressure and comparing it to a standard pressure level. Since atmospheric pressure decreases with altitude, the altimeter can calculate the aircraft's height above a reference level, usually sea level.

Why Altimeter Settings Matter

Accurate altimeter settings are vital for several reasons:

- Safety: Ensuring the aircraft flies at the correct altitude to avoid obstacles and other aircraft.

- Navigation: Helping pilots navigate accurately by maintaining the correct altitude over terrain.

- Compliance: Adhering to air traffic control instructions and maintaining separation from other aircraft.

Types of Altimeter Settings

There are several altimeter settings that pilots use during different phases of flight:

QNH

Definition:

QNH is the altimeter setting that pilots use to adjust their altimeter to show the altitude above sea level at a particular location. It accounts for the current atmospheric pressure at sea level.

Use:

Pilots use QNH during takeoff, landing, and when flying at lower altitudes. Setting the altimeter to QNH ensures that the altitude shown is the aircraft's height above sea level, which helps in avoiding terrain and obstacles.

Flight Instruments and Avionics | 93

QFE

Definition:

QFE is the altimeter setting that adjusts the altimeter to read zero when the aircraft is on the ground at the reference airfield.

Use:

QFE is used to show the height above the airfield. This setting is less common and is mainly used in certain regions and for specific operations like approaches and landings at that airfield.

QNE - Standard Pressure Setting

Definition:

The standard pressure setting is a fixed value used at higher altitudes, typically above the transition altitude (**which varies by country**).

Use:

Pilots switch to the standard pressure setting when flying at higher altitudes to ensure all aircraft are using the same reference. This helps maintain proper separation between aircraft.

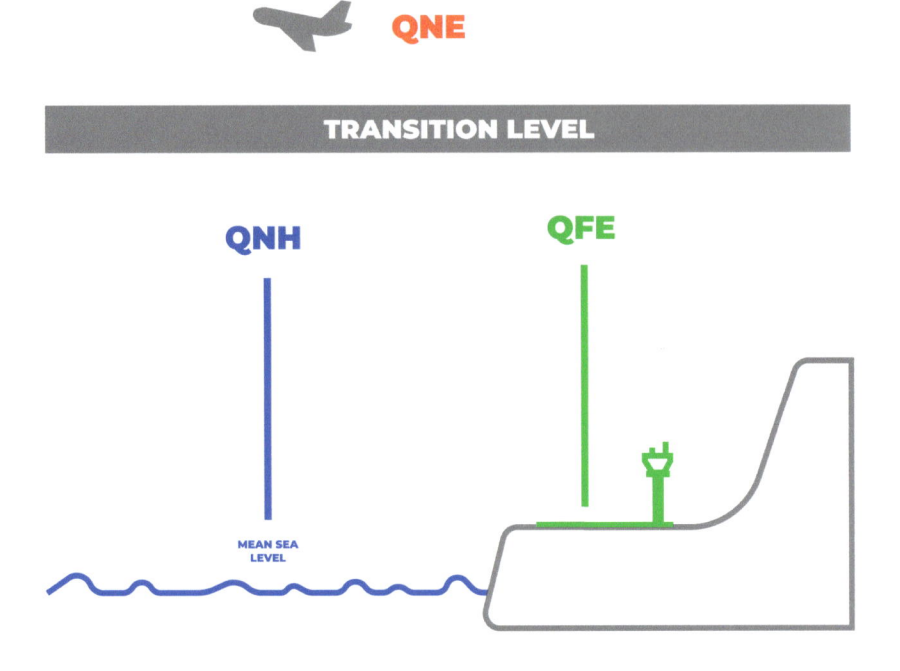

Transition Altitude and Level

The transition altitude is the altitude at which pilots change from using the local altimeter setting (**QNH**) to the standard pressure setting. This altitude varies by country but is typically around 18,000 feet in the United States.

- Below Transition Altitude: Use QNH for local altitude readings.
- Above Transition Altitude: Switch to the standard pressure setting.

When descending, pilots switch back to QNH at the transition level, which is slightly above the transition altitude to ensure a safe margin.

Chapter 5

Navigation and Flight Management

VOR Navigation

VHF Omnidirectional Range (**VOR**) is a critical radio navigation system used in aviation to provide precise azimuth information, helping pilots determine their position and maintain accurate course tracking. Understanding how VOR works and how to use it effectively is essential for safe and efficient navigation.

How VOR Works

VOR stations are ground-based radio transmitters that emit two types of signals: a reference signal and a variable signal. These signals work together to provide the pilot with directional information.

- **Reference Signal:** This is a continuous, omnidirectional signal that transmits at a constant frequency.

- **Variable Signal:** This signal rotates 360 degrees around the station and varies in phase depending on the direction from which it is received.

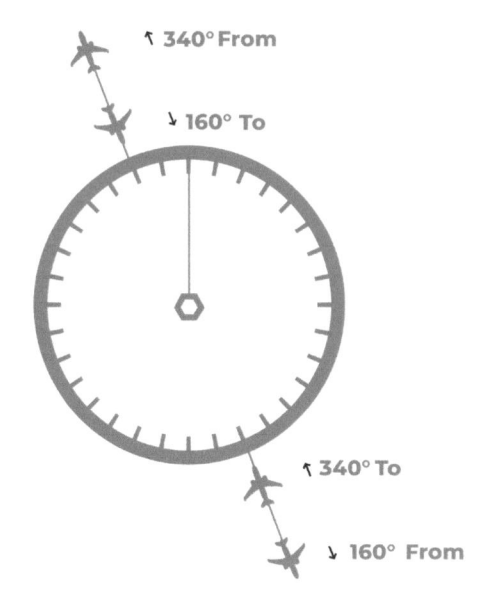

The aircraft's VOR receiver compares the phase of the received reference signal with the phase of the variable signal. The difference in phase corresponds to a specific radial (**bearing**) from the VOR station, which is measured in degrees from magnetic north, ranging from 0° to 359°.

For example, if the aircraft is on the 90° radial from the VOR station, the phase difference between the reference signal and the variable signal will correspond to 90°. This information is displayed on the aircraft's navigation instruments, typically on the Course Deviation Indicator (**CDI**) or Horizontal Situation Indicator (**HSI**).

Using VOR for Navigation

Tuning and Identifying the VOR Station:

- **Tune:** The pilot selects the desired VOR frequency on the navigation radio.
- **Identify:** The pilot listens to the Morse code identifier transmitted by the VOR station to ensure it is the correct station. This step is crucial to avoid navigation errors caused by tuning into the wrong station.

Setting and Intercepting a Radial:

- **Set the Course:** The pilot rotates the Omni-Bearing Selector (**OBS**) knob to set the desired radial on the navigation instrument.
- **Intercepting the Radial:** The aircraft is maneuvered to intercept the selected radial. The CDI needle will indicate whether the aircraft is left or right of the radial. The pilot adjusts the aircraft's heading to fly towards the radial until the CDI needle centers, indicating the aircraft is on the desired radial.

Tracking the Radial:

- Once on the radial, the pilot maintains the aircraft's position by making small heading adjustments to keep the CDI needle centered. This process requires continuous monitoring and correcting for wind drift to stay on course.

Determining Position Using Cross Radials:

- The pilot can use two VOR stations to determine the aircraft's position. By identifying the radials from two different VOR stations and plotting their intersection on a navigation chart, the exact position of the aircraft can be pinpointed. This technique is particularly useful for confirming location during flight.

Practical Applications of VOR

En-Route Navigation: VOR is widely used for en-route navigation along airways, which are predefined routes between VOR stations. Pilots use VOR radials to stay on course and ensure they are following the correct airway.

Instrument Approaches: Many instrument approach procedures rely on VOR for precise lateral guidance during the approach phase of flight, especially in poor visibility conditions.

Holding Patterns: VOR radials help in establishing and maintaining holding patterns, which are used for traffic management and delay handling.

Limitations of VOR

While VOR is a highly reliable and accurate navigation system, it has some limitations:

- **Line of Sight:** VOR signals require a clear line of sight between the aircraft and the station. Terrain, buildings, or the curvature of the Earth can obstruct the signal, especially at lower altitudes.
- **Signal Interference:** VOR signals can be affected by obstacles, atmospheric conditions, and equipment malfunctions, potentially leading to inaccurate readings.
- **Magnetic Variation:** VOR radials are based on magnetic north, which changes over time due to the Earth's magnetic field. Pilots and navigational charts must account for this variation to ensure accurate navigation.

Understanding the principles and proper usage of VOR is essential for pilots to navigate effectively and safely. Regular practice, combined with a solid grasp of VOR concepts, ensures that pilots can make the most of this valuable navigational aid.

Distance Measuring Equipment (DME)

Distance Measuring Equipment (**DME**) is a critical navigation tool in aviation that provides pilots with slant-range distance to a ground-based station. It is often paired with VOR (**VHF Omnidirectional Range**) or ILS (**Instrument Landing System**) to enhance situational awareness and precision during flight.

How DME Works

DME operates by measuring the time it takes for a radio signal to travel between the aircraft and a ground station. Here's a simplified explanation:

1. **Interrogation:** The aircraft's DME transceiver (**called an interrogator**) sends out pulsed radio signals (**UHF frequency, 962–1213 MHz**) to a ground-based DME station.
2. **Response:** The ground station (**a transponder**) receives these pulses and sends back a reply signal on a paired frequency.
3. **Calculation:** The DME unit calculates the distance by measuring the time delay between sending the interrogation and receiving the response.

Key Note: DME provides slant-range distance, not horizontal distance. At high altitudes or close proximity to the station, this creates a small error (**e.g., at 6 NM horizontally and 1 NM altitude, DME reads ~6.1 NM**).

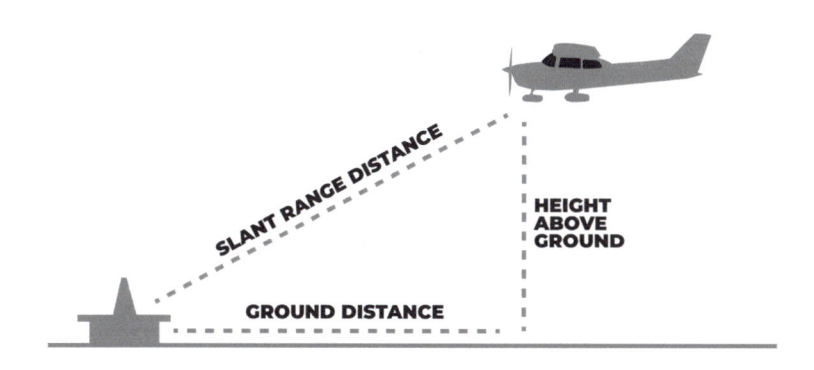

Navigation and Flight Management | 101

Components of DME

A DME system consists of two main parts:

1. **Airborne Unit:**

    - **Interrogator:** Sends pulses to the ground station.

    - **Display:** Shows distance (in NM) and sometimes ground speed/time-to-station.

2. **Ground Station:**

    - **Transponder:** Receives and replies to aircraft signals.

    - **Antenna:** Typically co-located with VOR or ILS for combined navigation (**e.g., VOR/DME or ILS/DME setups**).

Operating Modes

DME has three primary operating modes:

- **Search Mode:** Automatically scans for a valid ground station signal when first tuned.

- **Track Mode:** Locks onto the station and continuously updates distance.

- **Memory Mode:** Temporarily holds distance data if the signal is lost (useful in mountainous areas).

Practical Applications of DME

En-Route Navigation:

- Pilots use DME to confirm their position along airways or radial paths (**e.g., "25 NM northwest of ABC VOR/DME"**).

Approach and Landing:

- ILS/DME: Provides precise distance to the runway threshold during instrument approaches.

- DME Arcs: Pilots fly a curved path around a DME station at a constant distance (**e.g., 10 NM arc**).

Holding Patterns:

- DME defines holding fixes (**e.g., "Hold 15 NM east of XYZ DME"**).

Technical Limitations

- **Line-of-Sight Requirement:** DME signals travel in straight lines, so terrain or obstructions can block the signal.
- **Maximum Range:** Typically 200–250 NM, depending on altitude and station power.
- **Channel Saturation:** Each DME station can handle ~100 aircraft simultaneously. Beyond this, accuracy degrades.
- **Frequency Pairing:** DME channels are paired with VOR/ILS frequencies (**e.g., tuning to a VOR automatically selects its paired DME**).

DME vs. GPS

While GPS is more modern, DME remains vital due to:

- **Redundancy:** DME is unaffected by GPS jamming or satellite outages.
- **Precision:** Provides exact distance to a specific point, unlike GPS waypoints.
- **Integration:** Works seamlessly with legacy systems like VOR and ILS.

Example Scenario

Imagine flying a DME arc approach:

- Tune to the ABC VOR/DME frequency (**e.g., 113.5 MHz**).
- The DME display shows your distance from ABC.
- Fly a circular path at 15 NM from ABC while descending to intercept the final approach course.

DME is a reliable, precise tool for measuring distance in aviation. By understanding its principles, pilots can enhance navigation accuracy, execute complex procedures like DME arcs, and maintain safety even when GPS is unavailable. While technically sophisticated, its operation boils down to a simple concept: time = distance.

Non-Directional Beacon (NDB)

The Non-Directional Beacon (**NDB**) is one of the oldest navigation systems in aviation. It transmits non-directional radio signals that allow pilots to determine their bearing relative to a ground station. While largely supplemented by modern systems like GPS, NDBs remain in use in some regions, particularly for basic navigation and non-precision approaches.

How NDB Works

The NDB system consists of two main components:

Ground Station (NDB):

- Transmits continuous low-frequency (**LF**) or medium-frequency (**MF**) radio signals in the 190–1750 kHz range.

- Signals radiate in all directions (**hence "non-directional"**).

Aircraft Equipment (ADF – Automatic Direction Finder):

- Receives the NDB signal and displays the bearing to the station on a RMI (**Radio Magnetic Indicator**) or a traditional ADF gauge.

- The ADF needle always points toward the ground station, regardless of the aircraft's heading.

Example:

- If the ADF needle points to "0°," the aircraft is flying directly toward the station.

- At "90°," the station is to the aircraft's right.

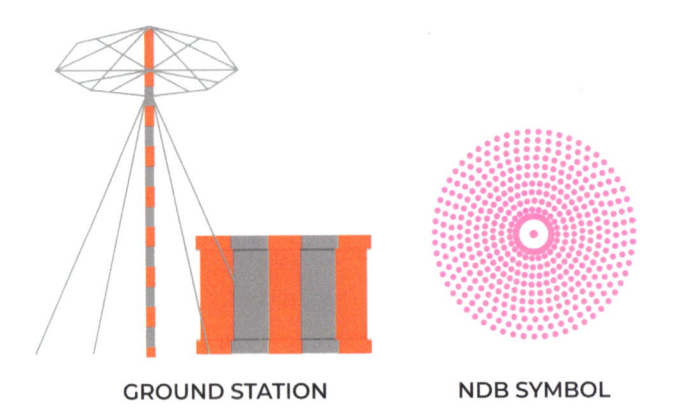

GROUND STATION   NDB SYMBOL

| Navigation and Flight Management

Practical Applications

En-Route Navigation:

- Pilots follow NDB signals to maintain a rough course between waypoints (**e.g., "Fly to NDB ‚ABC,' then proceed to NDB ‚XYZ'"**).

Non-Precision Approach:

- Simple instrument approaches where the NDB serves as a reference point. Pilots use the ADF to align with the runway.

Emergency Backup:

- Provides redundancy if modern systems (**e.g., GPS**) fail.

Technical Limitations

Signal Interference:

- NDB signals are prone to disruption from thunderstorms, mountains, or electronic interference.
- At night, "*skywave*" propagation can distort accuracy.

Limited Range:

- Typical range: 50–150 NM, depending on transmitter power and antenna height.

Accuracy Issues:

- The ADF shows relative bearing, not true course. Pilots must correct for wind drift and magnetic variation.
- Common errors include quadrantal error (**aircraft structure interference**) and coastal refraction (**signal bending over water**).

NDB vs. VOR/GPS Comparison

Feature	NDB/ADF	VOR/DME or GPS
Accuracy	Low (~5–10° error)	High (~1–2° error for VOR, <1m for GPS)
Range	50–150 NM	200+ NM (**VOR**), Global (**GPS**)
Reliability	Low (weather/terrain interference)	High (line-of-sight for VOR, satellite for GPS)
Cost	Low (simple infrastructure)	High (complex systems)

Example Scenario: NDB Approach

Setup:

- The pilot tunes the ADF to the NDB frequency (**e.g., 385 kHz for station "ABC"**).

Approach:

- The ADF needle points to the station. The pilot adjusts the heading to keep the needle at "0°."

Descent:

- At a predetermined distance (**from charts**), the pilot begins descending toward the runway.

Why NDBs Are Still Used

- **Cost-Effective:** Simple to install and maintain, especially in remote areas.
- **Backup Utility:** Critical redundancy for GPS outages or electrical failures.
- **Training Value:** Teaches foundational radio navigation skills to student pilots.

The NDB is a legacy navigation tool with declining but persistent relevance. While less precise than modern systems, its simplicity and reliability make it a valuable backup and training aid. Understanding NDB operations is essential for pilots to master basic radio navigation and handle emergencies.

ILS - (Instrument Landing System)

The Instrument Landing System (**ILS**) stands as a critical navigation aid for pilots during the approach and landing phase at airports worldwide. It is an advanced system that provides precise guidance information to aircraft, facilitating safe touchdown even in adverse weather conditions.

Comprising two primary components, the ILS includes the Localizer (**LOC**) and the Glide Slope (**GS**). The Localizer emits signals horizontally, directing the aircraft towards the runway centerline. Meanwhile, the Glide Slope offers vertical guidance to ensure an optimal descent path. Together, they furnish pilots with precise instructions to align the aircraft precisely with the runway and maintain the correct altitude.

Localizer

90 Hz
150 Hz

Glideslope

90 Hz
150 Hz

A typical ILS display in the cockpit presents pilots with information about the current course and altitude relative to the ideal glide path. This allows pilots to make necessary corrections to maintain the optimal approach trajectory.

The reliability of the ILS is paramount, particularly in adverse weather conditions such as heavy fog or rain, where visibility is limited. In such situations, the ILS provides pilots with the necessary reference points for a safe landing, irrespective of visual cues.

Navigation and Flight Management

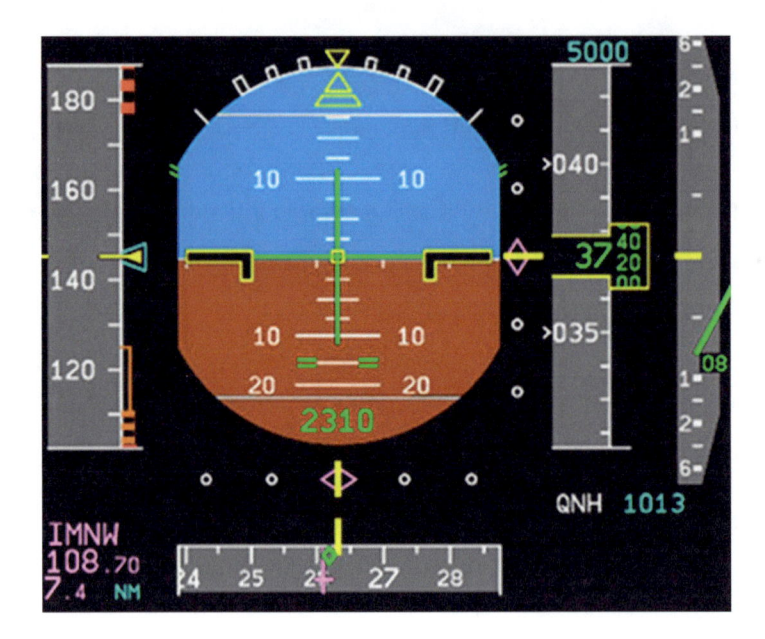

Thanks to its precision and reliability, the ILS has become an indispensable instrument for flight safety. It plays a crucial role in facilitating landings under various conditions, ensuring safe and efficient operations and significantly contributing to the smooth flow of air traffic.

Overall, the Instrument Landing System represents a milestone in aviation technology, substantially enhancing the safety and efficiency of landing operations and continuing to play a vital role in ensuring the safe operation of aircraft worldwide.

RNAV and LNAV

RNAV (**Area Navigation**) and LNAV (**Lateral Navigation**) are modern navigation systems that allow aircraft to fly flexible, precise routes without relying solely on ground-based navigation aids like VORs or NDBs. These systems have revolutionized aviation by enabling more efficient flight paths, reducing fuel consumption, and improving safety.

What is RNAV?

RNAV stands for Area Navigation. It allows aircraft to navigate along any desired flight path within the coverage of ground- or space-based navigation aids. Unlike traditional navigation, which requires flying directly to or from ground stations, RNAV enables pilots to create custom routes using waypoints defined by latitude and longitude.

How It Works:

- RNAV systems use data from multiple sources, such as GPS, DME, or VOR, to calculate the aircraft's position.
- Pilots or flight management systems (**FMS**) program a series of waypoints into the RNAV system, and the aircraft follows the route automatically.

Key Features:

- **Flexible Routing:** RNAV allows for direct point-to-point navigation, avoiding the need to follow fixed airways.
- **Precision:** RNAV systems provide highly accurate position information, often within a few meters.
- **Efficiency:** By enabling shorter routes, RNAV reduces flight time and fuel consumption.

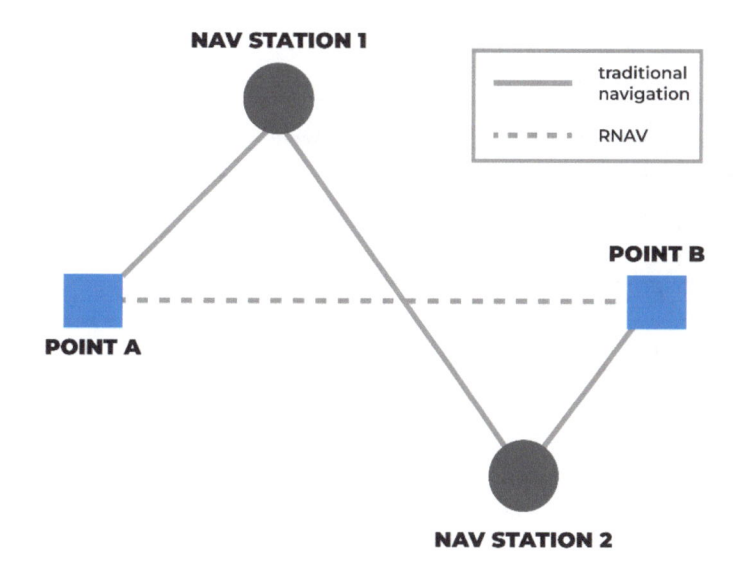

What is LNAV?

LNAV stands for Lateral Navigation. It is a component of RNAV that focuses on horizontal guidance (**left/right**) along a flight path. LNAV ensures the aircraft stays on the intended lateral track, while vertical guidance (**if needed**) is handled separately by systems like VNAV (**Vertical Navigation**).

Navigation and Flight Management | 109

How It Works:

- LNAV uses GPS or other navigation sources to guide the aircraft along a predefined lateral path.
- It is commonly used during en-route navigation and non-precision approaches.

Key Features:

- Lateral Precision: LNAV ensures the aircraft stays on the correct track, even in challenging conditions.
- Non-Precision Approaches: LNAV is often used for approaches where vertical guidance is not provided (**e.g., LNAV minima**).

RNAV vs. LNAV

Feature	RNAV	LNAV
Scope	Full area navigation (lateral + vertical)	Lateral navigation only
Guidance	Can include vertical guidance (VNAV)	Horizontal guidance only
Applications	En-route, approaches, departures	En-route, non-precision approaches

Types of RNAV

Basic RNAV (B-RNAV):

- Requires navigation accuracy of ±5 NM.
- Used in European airspace for en-route navigation.

Precision RNAV (P-RNAV):

- Requires navigation accuracy of ±1 NM.
- Used for terminal area operations and approaches.

Required Navigation Performance (RNP):

- A more advanced form of RNAV that includes onboard performance monitoring and alerting.
- RNP allows for operations in challenging environments, such as mountainous regions or curved approaches.

Benefits of RNAV and LNAV

Efficiency:

- Shorter routes and optimized flight paths save time and fuel.

Flexibility:

- RNAV allows for custom routes, reducing reliance on ground-based navigation aids.

Safety:

- Precise navigation reduces the risk of errors and enhances situational awareness.

Environmental Impact:

- Reduced fuel consumption lowers emissions, contributing to greener aviation.

RNAV and LNAV have transformed modern aviation by enabling flexible, precise, and efficient navigation. By understanding these systems, pilots can take full advantage of their capabilities, whether flying en-route, on approach, or during departures. RNAV and LNAV are essential tools for safe and efficient flight operations in today's airspace.

Vertical Navigation (VNAV)

Vertical Navigation (**VNAV**) is a critical component of modern flight management systems (**FMS**) that allows aircraft to follow precise vertical flight paths during climb, cruise, and descent. By automating altitude changes, VNAV enhances efficiency, reduces pilot workload, and ensures compliance with air traffic control (**ATC**) requirements.

What is VNAV?

VNAV stands for Vertical Navigation. It is a system that provides vertical guidance to pilots, ensuring the aircraft follows a predefined altitude profile. Unlike LNAV (**Lateral Navigation**), which controls the horizontal path, VNAV focuses on managing the aircraft's altitude and vertical speed.

How It Works:

- VNAV uses data from the aircraft's FMS, including flight plan waypoints, altitude restrictions, and performance parameters (**e.g., weight, speed, and wind**).
- It calculates the optimal climb, cruise, and descent profiles to meet ATC requirements and operational goals.
- Pilots can monitor and adjust the VNAV profile as needed.

Key Features:

- **Precision:** VNAV ensures the aircraft meets altitude restrictions at specific waypoints.
- **Efficiency:** Optimized climb and descent profiles reduce fuel consumption.
- **Automation:** Reduces pilot workload by automating altitude changes.

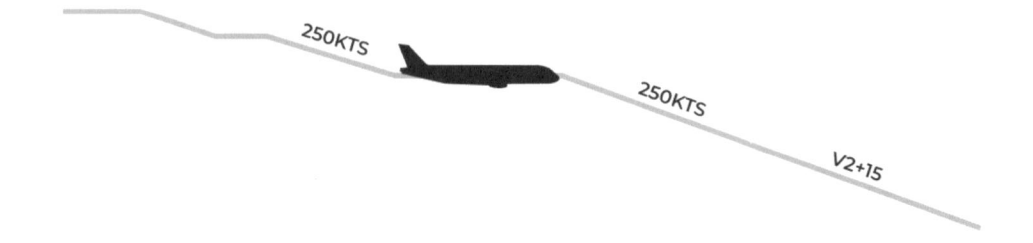

Components of VNAV

Flight Management System (FMS):

- The FMS is the brain of VNAV, calculating the vertical profile based on the flight plan and aircraft performance.

Altitude Restrictions:

- Waypoints often have altitude constraints (**e.g., "at or below 10,000 feet by WAYPOINT A"**). VNAV ensures these restrictions are met.

Vertical Speed and Thrust Management:

- VNAV adjusts the aircraft's vertical speed and engine thrust to achieve the desired profile.

Pilot Interface:

- Pilots can monitor the VNAV profile on the Primary Flight Display (**PFD**) or Navigation Display (**ND**) and make adjustments as needed.

Benefits of VNAV

Fuel Efficiency:

- Optimized climb and descent profiles reduce fuel consumption.

Environmental Impact:

- Continuous descents minimize noise and emissions near airports.

Safety:

- VNAV ensures compliance with altitude restrictions, reducing the risk of conflicts with other aircraft or terrain.

Pilot Workload Reduction:

- Automation of vertical navigation allows pilots to focus on other tasks.

VNAV is a cornerstone of modern aviation, enabling precise and efficient vertical navigation throughout all phases of flight. By automating altitude changes and optimizing flight profiles, VNAV enhances safety, reduces fuel consumption, and minimizes environmental impact.

Standard Instrument Departures (SIDs)

Standard Instrument Departures (SIDs) are predefined flight paths that aircraft follow immediately after takeoff. They are designed to ensure safe and efficient navigation from the airport to the en-route airspace. SIDs are crucial for managing air traffic, especially in busy airspace, and they help in noise abatement around airports.

Importance of SIDs

SIDs play a critical role in modern aviation by:

- Ensuring safe separation between departing aircraft.
- Providing a standardized procedure that all pilots can follow.
- Reducing the workload on air traffic controllers.
- Minimizing noise impact on surrounding communities.

Components of a SID Chart

Let's break down the components of a SID chart using the provided example from MARUN 3W:

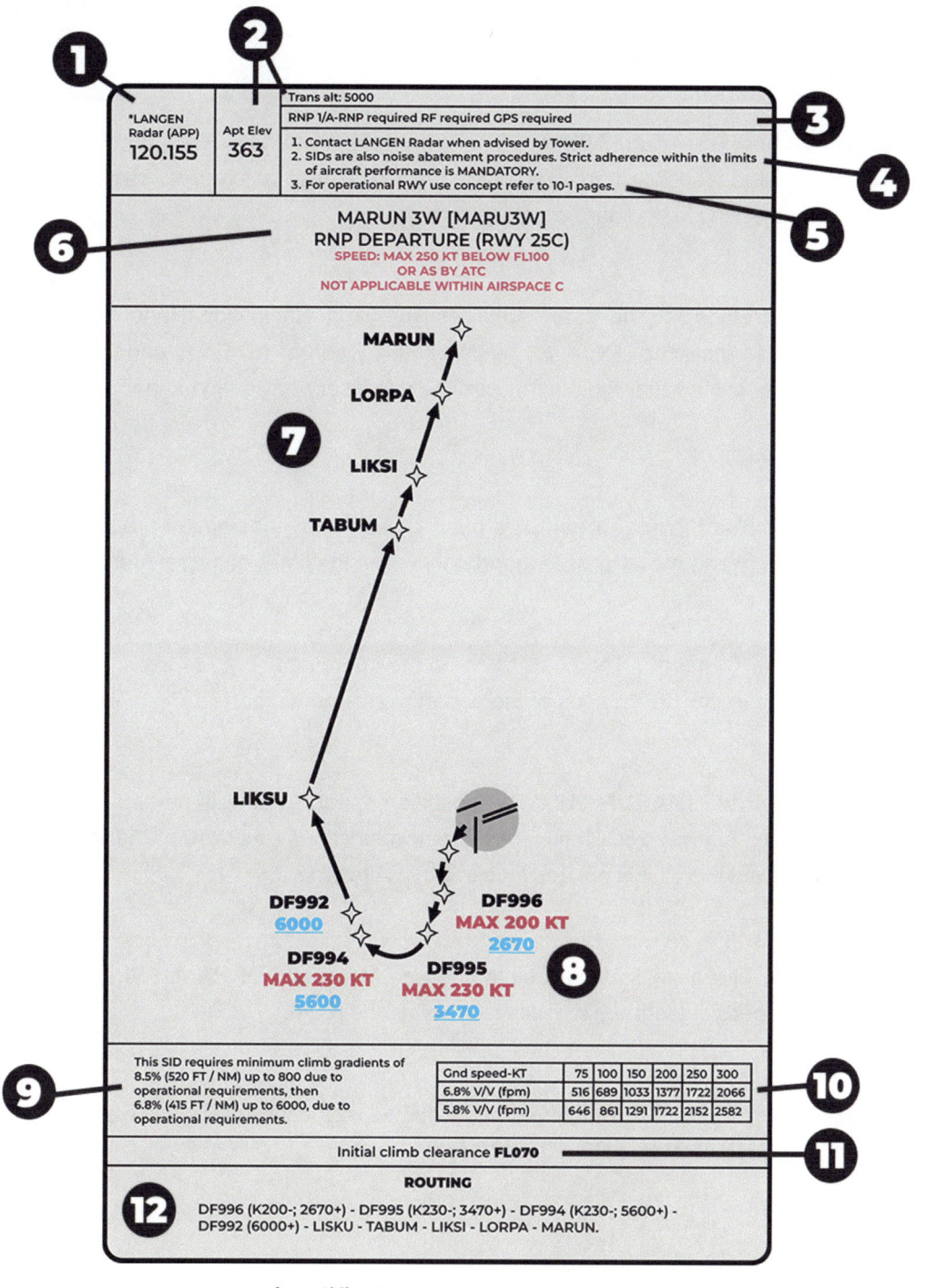

*LANGEN Radar (APP)
120.155

Apt Elev **363**

*Trans alt: 5000

RNP 1/A-RNP required RF required GPS required

1. Contact LANGEN Radar when advised by Tower.
2. SIDs are also noise abatement procedures. Strict adherence within the limits of aircraft performance is MANDATORY.
3. For operational RWY use concept refer to 10-1 pages.

MARUN 3W [MARU3W]
RNP DEPARTURE (RWY 25C)
SPEED: MAX 250 KT BELOW FL100
OR AS BY ATC
NOT APPLICABLE WITHIN AIRSPACE C

MARUN
LORPA
LIKSI
TABUM

LIKSU

DF992
6000

DF994
MAX 230 KT
5600

DF995
MAX 230 KT
3470

DF996
MAX 200 KT
2670

This SID requires minimum climb gradients of 8.5% (520 FT / NM) up to 800 due to operational requirements, then 6.8% (415 FT / NM) up to 6000, due to operational requirements.

Gnd speed-KT	75	100	150	200	250	300
6.8% V/V (fpm)	516	689	1033	1377	1722	2066
5.8% V/V (fpm)	646	861	1291	1722	2152	2582

Initial climb clearance **FL070**

ROUTING
DF996 (K200-; 2670+) - DF995 (K230-; 3470+) - DF994 (K230-; 5600+) - DF992 (6000+) - LISKU - TABUM - LIKSI - LORPA - MARUN.

Simplified SID Example Chart

Navigation and Flight Management | 115

1. **Radar and Communication:** The chart specifies the radar facility (**LANGEN Radar**) and the communication frequency (**120.155 MHz**). Pilots must contact LANGEN Radar as advised by the Tower.

2. **Elevation and Transition Altitude:** The airport elevation is 363 feet, and the transition altitude is 5000 feet. The transition altitude is the point at which pilots switch from local altitude references to standard pressure settings.

3. **RNP Requirements:** The chart specifies Required Navigation Performance (**RNP**) requirements, including RNP 1, A-RNP, RF (**Radius to Fix**), and GPS. These requirements ensure that the aircraft has the necessary navigation capabilities to follow the SID.

4. **Noise Abatement Procedures:** SIDs often include noise abatement procedures. Strict adherence to these procedures is mandatory within the limits of aircraft performance.

5. **Runway Use Concept:** The chart refers to the operational runway use concept, which can be found in the 10-IP pages of the airport's documentation.

6. **Departure Route (MARUN 3W):** The specific departure route is named MARUN 3W, applicable for Runway 25C. It includes speed restrictions (**maximum 250 knots below FL100**) and notes that it is not applicable within Airspace C.

7. **Waypoints:** The chart lists waypoints such as MARUN, LORPA, LIKSI, and TABUM. These are specific geographic points that define the route.

8. **Altitude Restrictions:** The chart provides altitude restrictions at various waypoints, such as DF996 (**2670 feet**) and DF995 (**3470 feet**).

9. **Climb Gradients:** The SID requires minimum climb gradients of 8.5% (**520 feet per nautical mile**) up to 800 feet, and then 6.8% (**415 feet per nautical mile**) up to 6000 feet. These gradients ensure that the aircraft gains altitude quickly enough to avoid obstacles and meet air traffic control requirements.

10. **Grid Speed and Vertical Speed:** The chart includes a grid that correlates ground speed (**in knots**) with the required vertical speed (**in feet per minute**) to achieve the specified climb gradients.

11. **Initial Climb Clearance:** The initial climb clearance is to FL070 (**7000 feet**).

12. **Routing:** The routing specifies the sequence of waypoints and altitude restrictions, such as DFP99 (**K200 ÷ 800+**), DFP98 (**K200 ÷ 1690+**), and so on, leading to the final waypoint MARUN.

Understanding and correctly interpreting SID charts is essential for pilots and air traffic controllers. These charts provide the necessary information for a safe and efficient departure from the airport. By following the predefined routes, altitudes, and speeds, pilots can ensure a smooth transition from the airport to the en-route airspace, contributing to overall flight safety and efficiency.

This chapter has provided a detailed overview of SIDs and how to interpret a SID chart using a real-world example. Mastery of this knowledge is crucial for anyone involved in aviation operations.

Standard Terminal Arrival Routes (STARs)

A Standard Terminal Arrival Route (**STAR**) is a predefined flight path that guides aircraft from the en-route phase of flight to the approach phase at an airport. STARs are designed to streamline traffic flow, enhance safety, and reduce pilot and air traffic controller workload.

What is a STAR?

A STAR is a published procedure that provides a transition from the en-route structure to the terminal area of an airport. It includes specific routes, altitudes, and speeds that pilots must follow to ensure safe and efficient arrival. STARs are especially important in busy airspace, where multiple aircraft are converging on a single airport.

Components of a STAR Chart

Let's break down the components of the provided STAR chart for WERRA 2P / WERRA 2R:

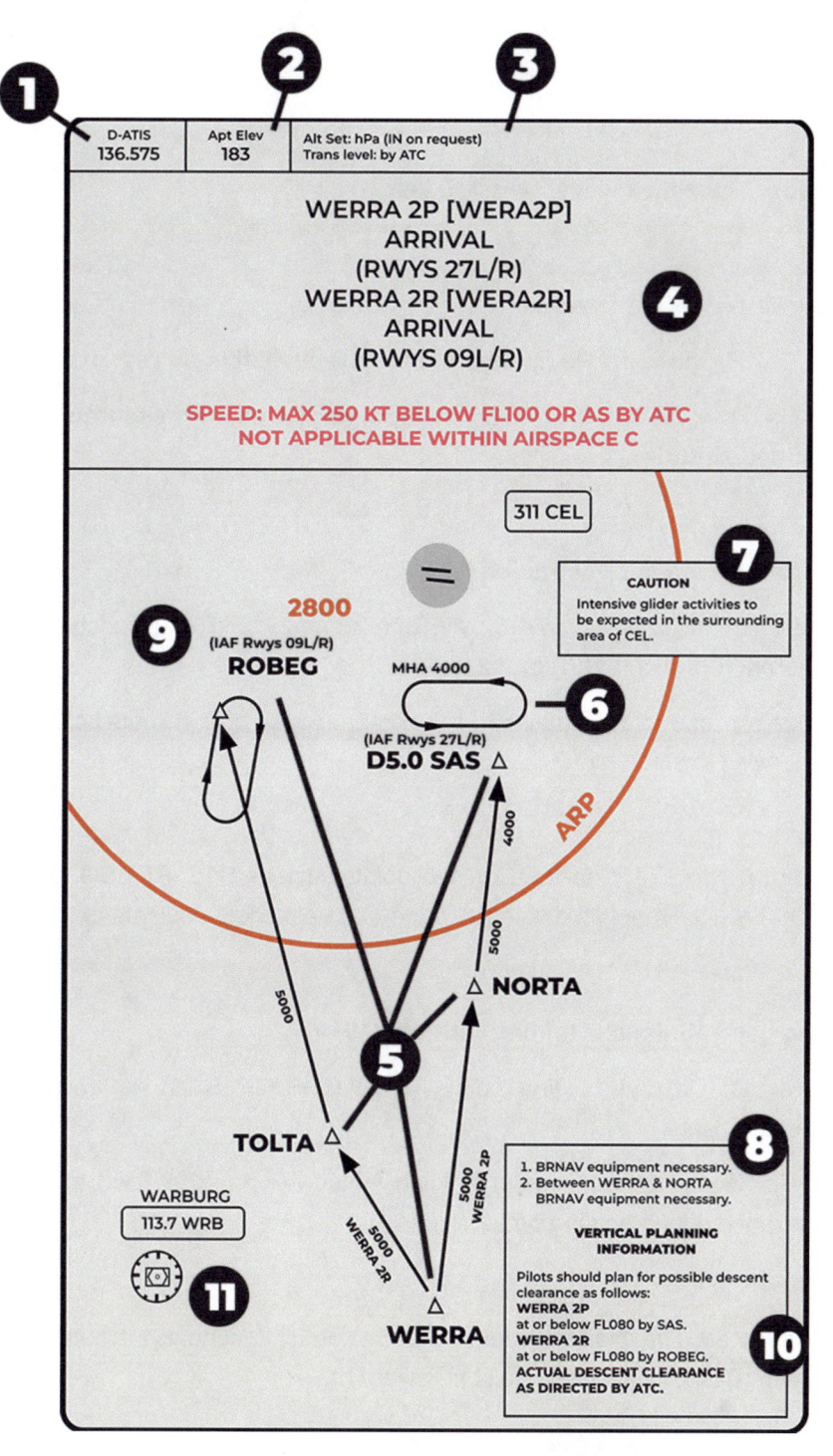

1	2	3
D-ATIS 136.575	Apt Elev 183	Alt Set: hPa (IN on request) Trans level: by ATC

**WERRA 2P [WERA2P]
ARRIVAL
(RWYS 27L/R)
WERRA 2R [WERA2R]
ARRIVAL
(RWYS 09L/R)**

**SPEED: MAX 250 KT BELOW FL100 OR AS BY ATC
NOT APPLICABLE WITHIN AIRSPACE C**

311 CEL

CAUTION
Intensive glider activities to be expected in the surrounding area of CEL.

2800
(IAF Rwys 09L/R)
ROBEG

MHA 4000

(IAF Rwys 27L/R)
D5.0 SAS

ARP

4000
5000

△ **NORTA**

5000

TOLTA △

5000 WERRA 2P

5000 WERRA 2R

WARBURG
113.7 WRB

△ **WERRA**

1. BRNAV equipment necessary.
2. Between WERRA & NORTA BRNAV equipment necessary.

VERTICAL PLANNING INFORMATION

Pilots should plan for possible descent clearance as follows:
WERRA 2P
at or below FL080 by SAS.
WERRA 2R
at or below FL080 by ROBEG.
ACTUAL DESCENT CLEARANCE AS DIRECTED BY ATC.

Simplified STAR Example Chart

Navigation and Flight Management | 119

1. **ATIS Frequency:** The frequency 136.575 is provided for the ATIS (**Automatic Terminal Information Service),** which gives pilots up-to-date information on weather, active runways, and other critical details.

2. **Elevation:** The airport elevation is 183 feet.

3. **Altitude & Transition Level:**
   - Alt Set: Provided in hPa (**inches of mercury available on request**).
   - Trans Level: Assigned by ATC (**ensures standardized pressure settings above a defined altitude**).

4. **STAR Name & Speed Restrictions:**
   - The chart includes two STARs: WERRA 2P and WERRA 2R, each corresponding to different runways (**09L/R and 27L/R**).
   - Pilots are instructed to maintain a maximum speed of 250 knots below FL100 unless otherwise directed by ATC.

5. **Waypoints:** The STAR includes key waypoints such as SAS, ROBEG, TOLTA, WERRA and NORTA. These points define the route and help pilots navigate to the airport.

6. **Holdings and Minimum Holding Altitude (MHA):**
   - Holdings: Defined holding points (**e.g., ROBEG, SAS**) are included for traffic management.
   - MHA: Specifies the Minimum Holding Altitude (**e.g., 4000 feet**) to ensure obstacle clearance during holding patterns.

7. **Caution Notes:** The chart includes important cautions, such as intensive glider activities near Celle (**CEL**), which pilots must be aware of.

8. **Navigation Requirements:** BRNAV (**Basic Area Navigation**) equipment is required between certain waypoints (**e.g., WERRA and NORTA**).

9. **Runway-Specific Information:** The STARs are tailored for specific runways (**09L/R and 27L/R**), with different initial approach fixes (**IAFs**) such as ROBEG for runways 09L/R and SAS for runways 27L/R.

10. **Altitude Restrictions:** Vertical planning information is provided, such as descending to FL080 by SAS for WERRA 2P or FL080 by ROBEG for WERRA 2R.

11. **VORs (VHF Omnidirectional Range):** VOR stations (**e.g., WARBURG 113.7**) are included as navigation aids. Pilots use VOR radials to align with the STAR route and verify their position.

How to Fly a STAR

Preparation:

- Before the flight, review the STAR chart and note key waypoints, altitude restrictions, and communication frequencies.
- Ensure the aircraft's navigation system is programmed with the STAR waypoints.

En-Route Transition:

- As you approach the terminal area, ATC will clear you to follow the STAR.
- Begin following the published route, adhering to altitude and speed restrictions.

Descent Planning:

- Plan your descent according to the vertical planning information. For example, on WERRA 2P, plan to be at or below FL080 by SAS.

Communication:

- Tune in to the ATIS frequency (**136.575**) to obtain current airport information.
- Maintain contact with ATC and report passing key waypoints.
- Be prepared for further instructions, such as vectoring for the final approach.

Importance of STARs

STARs play a critical role in modern aviation by:

- **Enhancing Safety:** Standardized routes reduce the risk of mid-air collisions.
- **Improving Efficiency:** Streamlined traffic flow reduces delays and fuel consumption.
- **Reducing Workload:** Predefined procedures simplify coordination between pilots and ATC.

STARs are essential tools for managing the transition from en-route to terminal airspace. By understanding how to read and follow STAR charts, pilots can ensure safe, efficient, and compliant arrivals at their destination airports.

Holdings

A holding pattern is a procedure used by aircraft when they need to delay their arrival at a destination or specific point in the airspace. Pilots enter a holding pattern to maintain safe separation from other aircraft or to wait until it is safe to proceed with their approach or route. Holding patterns are like invisible loops in the sky, where aircraft "hold" their position by flying in a defined, circular path. Holding patterns are usually assigned by air traffic control (**ATC**) when there is traffic congestion, poor weather conditions, or unexpected delays. They ensure that multiple planes can safely wait their turn to land or proceed on their routes.

The Structure of a Holding Pattern

A standard holding pattern resembles an oval-shaped racetrack.

It consists of *two main legs*:

Inbound Leg: This is the path flown toward a navigational fix (**a specific point in the air, such as a VOR station or GPS waypoint**).

Outbound Leg: This is the path flown away from the fix.

Each leg is typically one minute long when flying at or below 14,000 feet. Above 14,000 feet, each leg is typically one and a half minutes long.

The pattern also includes *two 180-degree turns*:

Entry Turn: A turn that helps the aircraft enter the holding pattern.

Exit Turn: A turn that leads the aircraft back toward the fix on the inbound leg.

The aircraft always flies the pattern with a right-hand turn unless instructed otherwise by ATC. This is called a standard holding pattern. If the turns are to the left, it is called a non-standard holding pattern.

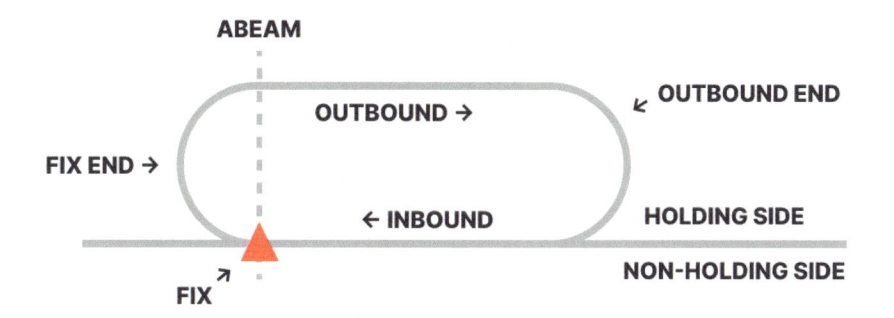

Why Do Pilots Use Holding Patterns?

Holding patterns are used for several reasons, including:

Traffic Delays: If there are too many planes arriving at an airport, ATC may ask aircraft to hold until there is space to land.

Bad Weather: If weather conditions make it unsafe to land, planes may hold until the weather improves.

Instrument Approaches: During instrument flight rules (**IFR**) operations, holding patterns help aircraft sequence safely before starting an approach.

Emergency Situations: If an emergency occurs, a holding pattern can give pilots more time to manage the situation or receive instructions from ATC.

Holding Pattern Entries

When a pilot is told to enter a holding pattern, they need to determine the best way to join the pattern. There are three types of holding entries that depend on the aircraft's direction of approach:

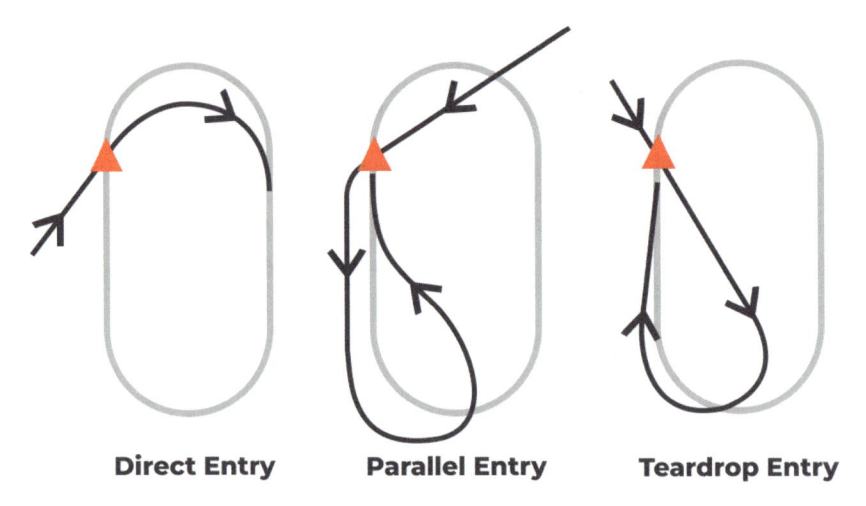

Direct Entry **Parallel Entry** **Teardrop Entry**

1. Direct Entry

This is the simplest entry. If the aircraft is approaching the holding fix in a way that aligns with the inbound leg, the pilot simply turns right (**in a standard hold**) to join the pattern directly.

2. Parallel Entry

This entry is used when the aircraft approaches the holding fix from an angle that does not align with the inbound leg. After crossing the fix, the pilot flies parallel to the holding pattern's outbound leg for one minute, then turns back to rejoin the pattern.

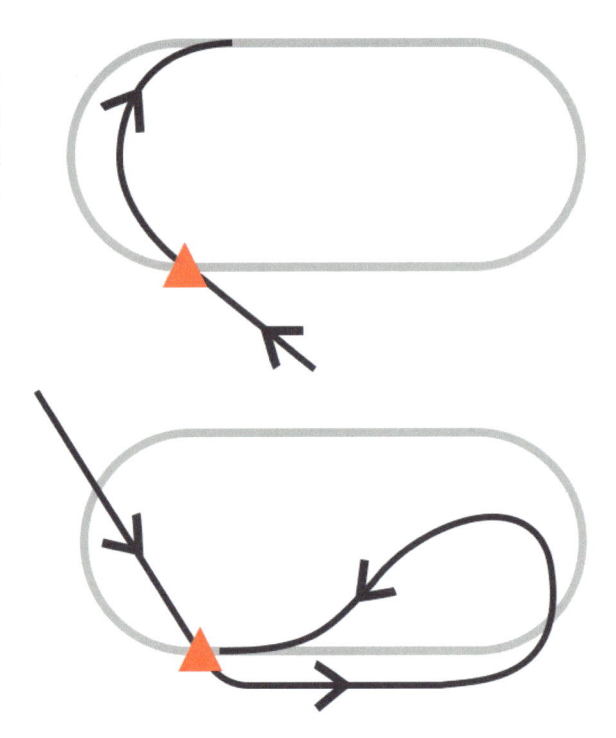

124 | **Navigation and Flight Management**

3. Teardrop Entry

This entry is used when the aircraft approaches the holding fix at an angle that is slightly more aligned with the outbound leg. After crossing the fix, the pilot turns 30 degrees away from the holding pattern, flies for one minute, and then turns back 180 degrees to rejoin the inbound leg.

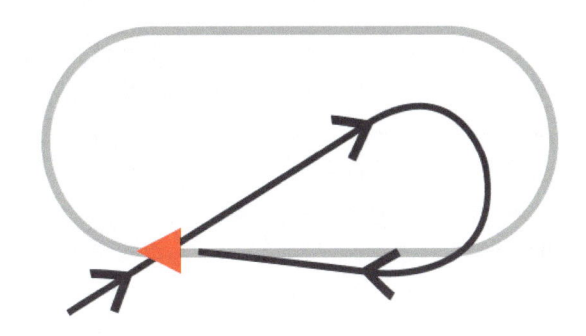

Tips for Flying Holding Patterns

Use Timers: Always use a timer to ensure each leg is flown for the correct duration (**one minute or one and a half minutes**).

Monitor Your Speed: Maintain the correct holding speed to avoid overshooting or undershooting the turns. Holding speeds are usually:

- 200 knots or less below 6,000 feet
- 230 knots between 6,000 and 14,000 feet
- 265 knots above 14,000 feet

Stay Calm: Holding patterns are routine procedures. Follow your training and communicate with ATC as needed.

Use Navigation Aids: Rely on instruments like VOR or GPS to help you stay on track during the hold.

Holding patterns are essential tools for managing air traffic safely and efficiently. They might seem complicated at first, but with practice, they become a normal part of flight operations. Knowing how to correctly enter and fly a holding pattern will make you a more confident and capable pilot.

True Heading vs. Magnetic Heading

Understanding the difference between true heading and magnetic heading is fundamental for pilots navigating in various flight conditions. Both headings are crucial for accurate navigation and flight planning, and they play a significant role in ensuring that aircraft follow their intended routes safely and efficiently. In aviation, a heading is the direction in which an aircraft's nose is pointed during flight. There are two primary types of headings: true heading and magnetic heading. Both are measured in degrees, but they reference different directional baselines.

True Heading

True heading is the direction in which the aircraft is pointed relative to true north, which is the geographic North Pole. It is an important reference for navigation, especially when dealing with flight plans and long-distance travel.

- **True North:** True north refers to the direction along the Earth's surface towards the geographic North Pole. Unlike magnetic north, true north is fixed and does not change.
- **Calculation:** True heading is typically determined using maps or GPS systems that reference the Earth's geographic coordinates.

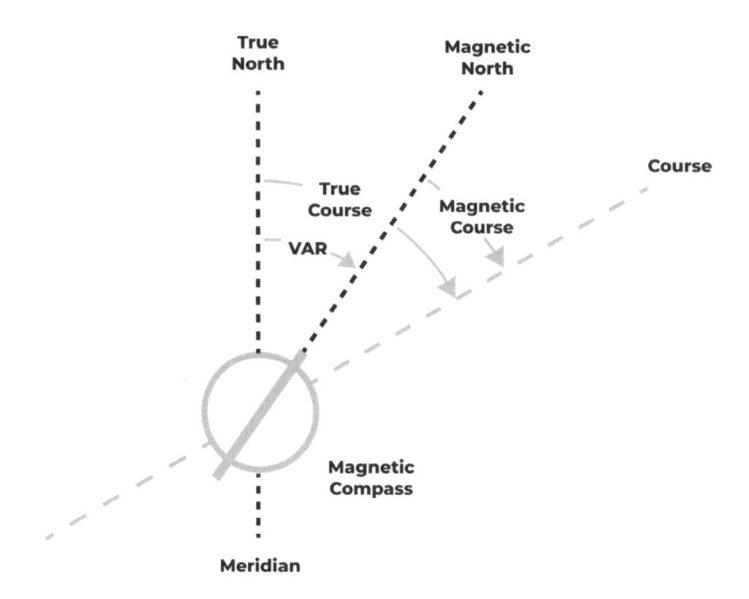

Magnetic Heading

Magnetic heading is the direction in which the aircraft is pointed

relative to magnetic north, which is the direction that a magnetic compass points. Magnetic north is different from true north because it is based on the Earth's magnetic field, which changes over time and varies depending on geographic location.

- **Magnetic North:** Magnetic north is the direction that the needle of a magnetic compass points, which is influenced by the Earth's magnetic field.

- **Calculation:** Magnetic heading is read directly from the aircraft's magnetic compass. Pilots often use magnetic heading because magnetic compasses are simple and reliable, even though magnetic north can shift due to changes in the Earth's magnetic field.

Magnetic Variation (Declination)

The difference between true north and magnetic north is known as magnetic variation or declination. This variation is specific to geographic locations and is expressed in degrees east or west.

- **East Variation:** When magnetic north is east of true north, the variation is considered east. To convert a true heading to a magnetic heading, subtract the variation.

- **West Variation:** When magnetic north is west of true north, the variation is considered west. To convert a true heading to a magnetic heading, add the variation.

For example, if the true heading is 100° and the magnetic variation is 10° west, the magnetic heading would be 110°.

Conversely, if the variation were 10° east, the magnetic heading would be 90°.

Using True and Magnetic Headings in Flight

Pilots use both true and magnetic headings for different purposes:

- **True Heading for Flight Planning:** True heading is primarily used in flight planning and when working with aeronautical charts. Charts and GPS systems often reference true north, making it essential for planning routes, especially for long-distance flights.
- **Magnetic Heading for In-Flight Navigation:** During flight, pilots typically use magnetic heading for real-time navigation because aircraft instruments, like the magnetic compass and heading indicator, are calibrated to magnetic north. This allows for straightforward and immediate directional reference.

Converting Between True and Magnetic Headings

Converting between true and magnetic headings requires knowledge of the local magnetic variation. The formula is straightforward:

- **True to Magnetic:** Magnetic Heading = True Heading ± Variation
- **Magnetic to True:** True Heading = Magnetic Heading ± Variation

The variation is added or subtracted based on whether it is east or west, respectively. This conversion is essential when transitioning from planning phases (where true headings are often used) to actual flight (where magnetic headings are used).

Practical Considerations

Updating Charts: Magnetic variation changes over time, so it is crucial to use updated aeronautical charts and data to ensure accuracy in navigation.

Regional Differences: Magnetic variation can be significantly different depending on the geographic location. Pilots must be aware of the variation in the regions they are flying over.

Instrument Checks: Regular checks and calibration of navigational instruments ensure that the headings read correctly and accurately reflect the intended direction.

Navigation on Earth

Understanding meridians, parallels, and how coordinates are made is important for navigation. These tools help in finding exact locations, planning routes, and ensuring accurate travel whether on land, sea, or in the air.

1. Introduction to Earth's Grid System

The Earth's grid system is a network of imaginary lines on the globe. It helps locate any point on the surface. This system is made up of meridians (**lines of longitude**) and parallels (**lines of latitude**). Together, they form the coordinate system used in navigation.

2. Meridians (Lines of Longitude)

Meridians are imaginary lines that run from the North Pole to the South Pole. They measure degrees of longitude, which tells how far east or west a location is from the Prime Meridian.

- **Prime Meridian:** The Prime Meridian is the zero-degree longitude line, running through Greenwich, England. It divides the Earth into the Eastern and Western Hemispheres.

- **Degrees of Longitude:** Longitude is measured in degrees (°), minutes ('), and seconds ("). The Prime Meridian is 0°, and longitude goes up to 180° east and 180° west.

- **Convergence at Poles:** Meridians meet at the poles, so the distance between them gets smaller as they move from the equator towards the poles.

3. Parallels (Lines of Latitude)

Parallels are imaginary lines that run parallel to the equator. They measure degrees of latitude, which tells how far north or south a location is from the equator.

- **Equator:** The equator is the zero-degree latitude line, equally distant from the North and South Poles. It divides the Earth into the Northern and Southern Hemispheres.

- **Degrees of Latitude:** Latitude is measured in degrees (°), minutes ('), and seconds ("). The equator is 0°, with latitude going up to 90° north (**North Pole**) and 90° south (**South Pole**).

- **Equal Distance:** Parallels stay the same distance apart across the globe, unlike meridians which come together at the poles.

Navigation and Flight Management

North Pole

Prime Meridian

Equator

South Pole

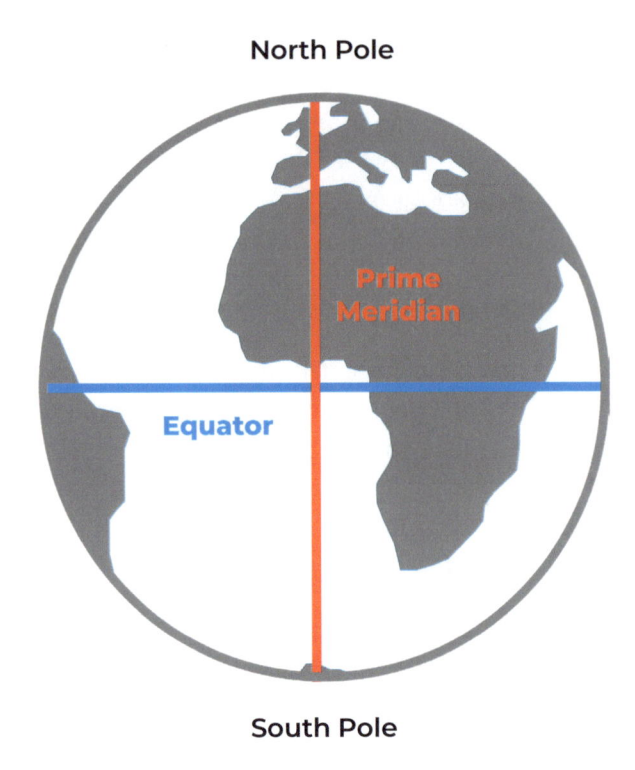

4. Coordinates and Their Formation

Coordinates are a set of values that define a specific point on the Earth's surface. They are expressed in terms of latitude and longitude, providing a precise way to identify locations.

- **Latitude and Longitude:** A coordinate is written as (**latitude, longitude**). For example, the coordinates for New York City are about 40.7128° N (**latitude**), 74.0060° W (**longitude**).

5. Reading Coordinates

Coordinates are usually given in degrees, minutes, and seconds to provide exact locations. Here's how to read them:

- **Degrees (°):** The largest unit. Each degree is divided into 60 minutes.
- **Minutes ('):** Each minute is one-sixtieth of a degree. Each minute is divided into 60 seconds.
- **Seconds (''):** The smallest unit of measure, each second is one-sixtieth of a minute.

For example, the coordinates *48° 51' 24" N, 2° 21' 8" E* can be broken down as follows:

- **Latitude:** 48 degrees, 51 minutes, 24 seconds north of the equator.
- **Longitude:** 2 degrees, 21 minutes, 8 seconds east of the Prime Meridian.

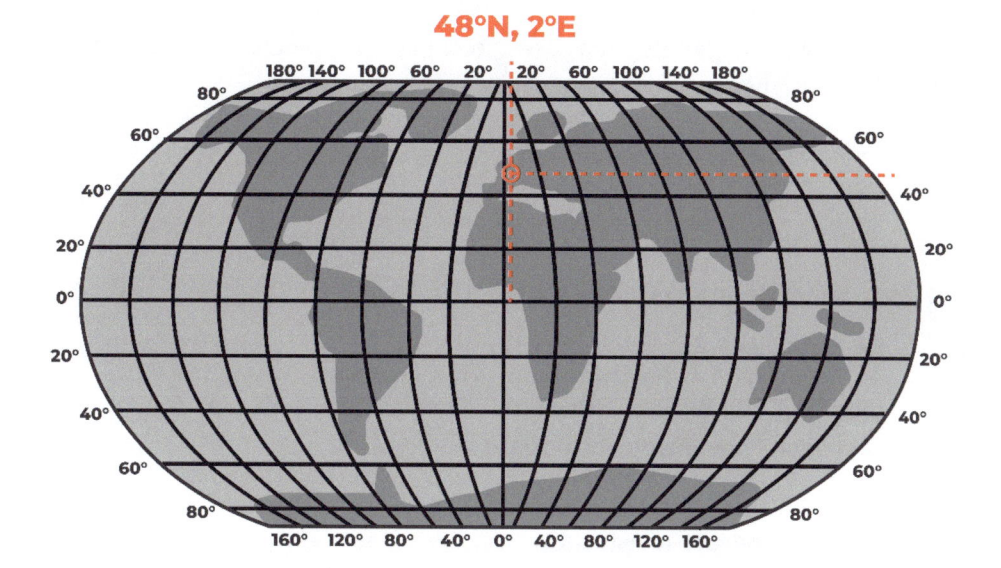

6. Decimal Degrees

For simplicity, coordinates can also be expressed in decimal degrees. This is often used in digital maps and GPS devices. For example:

- 48.8566° N, 2.3522° E.

To convert from degrees, minutes, and seconds to decimal degrees:

1. Divide the minutes by 60.
2. Divide the seconds by 3600.
3. Add these values to the degrees.

For example, to convert 48° 51' 24" N:

- 51' ÷ 60 = 0.85
- 24" ÷ 3600 ≈ 0.0067
- Total: 48 + 0.85 + 0.0067 ≈ 48.8567°

Navigation and Flight Management

7. Practical Use of Coordinates in Navigation

Coordinates are crucial in various forms of navigation:

- **Aviation:** Pilots use coordinates to create flight plans, ensuring accurate routes from departure to destination. GPS systems in aircraft rely on coordinates for real-time positioning.

- **Maritime Navigation:** Ships use coordinates to navigate the oceans, plotting courses that avoid hazards and ensure timely arrivals at ports.

- **Land Navigation:** Hikers, surveyors, and geographers use coordinates for precise location identification and mapping.

8. Importance of Accurate Coordinates

Accurate coordinates are vital for safety and efficiency in navigation. They help in:

- **Avoiding Obstacles:** Precise coordinates ensure that navigational routes avoid natural and man-made obstacles.

- **Search and Rescue:** In emergencies, exact coordinates allow for quick and efficient location of people in distress.

- **Global Positioning Systems (GPS):** GPS technology relies on accurate coordinates to provide real-time location data, essential for modern navigation.

Understanding meridians, parallels, and the coordinate system is essential for navigation on Earth. These tools provide a structured way to identify precise locations, plan routes, and ensure accurate travel. Whether in aviation, maritime, or land navigation, the ability to read and use coordinates is a key skill that enhances safety and efficiency in all navigational activities. By learning these concepts, navigators can confidently find their way and reach their destinations accurately.

How a Flight Route is Structured

A well-planned flight route is essential for safe and efficient air travel. Whether for a short domestic flight or a long international journey, the structure of a flight route involves careful consideration of various factors, including airspace restrictions, weather conditions, and the aircraft's capabilities. Understanding how a flight route is built helps pilots navigate smoothly from departure to arrival.

1. Flight Route Overview

A flight route is a predetermined path that an aircraft follows from the departure airport to the destination. It consists of several key elements, including waypoints, airways, and navigation aids. The route ensures that the flight adheres to air traffic control (**ATC**) regulations, avoids hazards, and optimizes fuel efficiency.

2. Departure Procedures

The flight begins with departure procedures, which are designed to guide the aircraft safely from the airport to the en-route phase. These procedures typically include:

- **Standard Instrument Departure (SID):** A predefined route used by IFR aircraft to depart from an airport, ensuring safe clearance of obstacles and efficient traffic management. SIDs provide guidance on altitude, direction, and waypoints to follow after takeoff.

- **Initial Climb:** After takeoff, the aircraft climbs to a specified altitude, following the SID or instructions from ATC, to integrate smoothly into the en-route airspace.

Navigation and Flight Management | 133

3. En-Route Phase

The en-route phase is the longest part of the flight, where the aircraft cruises at a high altitude towards the destination. Key components of this phase include:

- **Airways:** These are pre-defined corridors in the sky, similar to highways on the ground, that guide aircraft from one point to another. Airways are established to ensure safe and efficient traffic flow, often following specific navigation aids like VOR stations.
- **Waypoints:** Waypoints are specific geographical locations, often defined by latitude and longitude, that the aircraft passes over during the flight. They are used to define the flight path and ensure that the aircraft stays on course. Waypoints can be fixed points on an airway or independently located in the sky.
- **Navigation Aids (NAVAIDs):** These are ground-based or satellite-based systems that assist in navigation. Common NAVAIDs include VOR (**Very High-Frequency Omnidirectional Range**), NDB (**Non-Directional Beacon**), and GPS (Global Positioning System). Pilots use these aids to follow the flight route accurately.
- **Cruising Altitude:** During the en-route phase, the aircraft reaches and maintains a cruising altitude, which is typically between 30,000 and 40,000 feet for commercial flights. The altitude is selected based on optimal fuel efficiency, weather conditions, and air traffic.

4. Airspace Considerations

While planning a flight route, pilots must consider the different types of airspace they will be flying through. This includes:

- **Controlled Airspace:** The flight must adhere to ATC instructions, especially when passing through busy airspace classes like B, C, or D.
- **Special Use Airspace:** Routes may need to avoid restricted or prohibited areas, such as military operations areas or airspace over sensitive locations.
- **Oceanic and Remote Airspace:** For transoceanic flights, pilots follow specific oceanic tracks and procedures, as these areas have limited radar and communication coverage.

5. Arrival Procedures

As the aircraft approaches the destination, arrival procedures guide it from the en-route phase to a safe landing. These procedures include:

- **Standard Terminal Arrival Route (STAR):** Similar to SIDs, STARs are predefined routes that guide aircraft from the en-route phase to the approach phase. They help manage traffic flow into busy airports and ensure that aircraft arrive at the correct position for landing.
- **Approach Phase:** The aircraft transitions from cruise to descent, following the STAR and any additional ATC instructions. This phase often includes aligning with the final approach course using an Instrument Landing System (**ILS**), VOR, or GPS, depending on the airport and weather conditions.
- **Final Approach:** The final part of the approach where the aircraft aligns with the runway and prepares for landing. The pilot follows precise instructions to ensure a safe descent and touchdown.

6. Alternate Routes and Diversions

A well-structured flight route also includes planning for alternate routes and potential diversions. These considerations are crucial for ensuring safety in case of unexpected events, such as:

- **Weather Changes:** Pilots may need to alter the route if severe weather conditions develop along the planned path.
- **Technical Issues:** If the aircraft experiences technical problems, the pilot may need to divert to an alternate airport that was pre-planned during the route planning process.
- **Traffic Management:** ATC may direct pilots to take a different route or hold at a waypoint to manage traffic congestion or other airspace considerations.

FMS - Flight Management System

The Flight Management System (**FMS**) is a vital component of modern aviation, providing pilots with essential tools to manage and optimize flight operations. This chapter explores the FMS, detailing its functions, components, and significance in contemporary aircraft.

What is the Flight Management System (FMS)?

The Flight Management System is an integrated system used to automate a wide variety of in-flight tasks, thereby reducing the workload on pilots and increasing the efficiency and safety of flight operations. The FMS encompasses several subsystems and interfaces with various avionics components to ensure seamless control over flight planning, navigation, performance management, and aircraft guidance.

Key Functions of the FMS:

Flight Planning

The FMS allows pilots to create, store, and manage flight plans. It calculates optimal routes based on various factors such as weather, airspace restrictions, and aircraft performance. This includes determining waypoints, airways, and approach procedures.

Navigation

The FMS integrates data from multiple navigation sources, including GPS, INS (**Inertial Navigation System**), and VOR (**VHF Omnidirectional Range**) to provide accurate positioning and navigation information. It guides the aircraft along the planned route, automatically adjusting for any deviations.

Performance Management

The system calculates critical performance parameters such as fuel consumption, optimal speeds, and altitudes. It assists in managing the aircraft's engines and other systems to ensure efficient fuel usage and adherence to performance limits.

Aircraft Guidance

The FMS interfaces with the autopilot and flight director systems to provide automatic lateral and vertical guidance. This includes controlling the aircraft during climbs, cruises, descents, and approaches, as well as executing complex maneuvers like holding patterns and missed approaches.

Components of the FMS:

Control Display Unit (CDU)

The CDU is the primary interface through which pilots interact with the FMS. It consists of a display screen and a keyboard or touch interface, allowing pilots to input data, view flight information, and make adjustments to the flight plan.

Flight Management Computer (FMC)

The FMC is the central processing unit of the FMS. It processes input data, performs calculations, and manages the execution of the flight plan. The FMC integrates information from various sensors and systems to provide accurate navigation and performance data.

Database

The FMS database contains essential information such as navigation data (**waypoints, airways, navaids**), airport data (**runways, taxiways, gates**), and aircraft performance data. This database is regularly updated to ensure the accuracy and currency of the information.

Significance of the FMS:

Enhanced Efficiency

By automating many of the tasks traditionally performed by pilots, the FMS increases operational efficiency. It optimizes flight paths and fuel consumption, leading to cost savings and reduced environmental impact.

Increased Safety

The FMS enhances flight safety by providing precise navigation and performance data, reducing the likelihood of human error. It ensures compliance with air traffic control instructions and adherence to safety protocols.

Reduced Pilot Workload

The FMS significantly reduces the workload on pilots, allowing them to focus on monitoring the flight and managing any anomalies or emergencies. This leads to better situational awareness and decision-making.

Consistency and Accuracy

The FMS ensures consistent and accurate execution of flight plans, reducing variability and improving the predictability of flight operations. This is particularly important in busy airspace and complex flight environments.

The Flight Management System is a cornerstone of modern aviation, transforming the way flights are planned and managed. Its integration of advanced technologies and automation capabilities enhances efficiency, safety, and reliability in flight operations. Understanding the functions and components of the FMS is essential for pilots and aviation professionals, as it plays a critical role in the successful operation of contemporary aircraft.

Chapter 6

Meteorology for Aviators

Layers of the Atmosphere

Understanding the layers of the atmosphere is fundamental for anyone involved in aviation. The Earth's atmosphere is a complex, multi-layered envelope of gases that not only protects life on Earth but also plays a crucial role in aviation. The atmosphere is divided into several distinct layers, each with its own characteristics and significance for flight operations. This chapter explores these layers, their properties, and their impact on aviation.

1. Troposphere

Characteristics

- **Altitude Range:** Surface to approximately 8-15 kilometers (**5-9 miles**)
- **Temperature:** Decreases with altitude, about 6.5°C per kilometer
- **Composition:** Contains approximately 75% of the atmosphere's mass and nearly all water vapor

Significance for Aviation

The troposphere is the lowest layer of the atmosphere and is where virtually all weather phenomena occur, including clouds, rain, and storms. This layer is highly turbulent, affecting flight operations, particularly during takeoff and landing. Pilots must be well-versed in interpreting weather patterns in the troposphere to ensure safe flight operations.

2. Stratosphere

Characteristics

- **Altitude Range:** 15 to 50 kilometers (**9 to 31 miles**)
- **Temperature:** Increases with altitude due to the absorption of ultraviolet (**UV**) radiation by the ozone layer
- **Composition:** Contains the ozone layer, which absorbs and scatters UV solar radiation

Significance for Aviation

The stratosphere is critical for high-altitude flight. Commercial jet aircraft typically cruise in the lower stratosphere (**around 10-12 kilometers**) where the air is more stable and less turbulent than in the troposphere. The reduced turbulence and lower air density result in smoother flights and improved fuel efficiency. However, pilots must be aware of potential threats such as clear air turbulence (**CAT**) which can occur in this layer.

3. Mesosphere

Characteristics

- **Altitude Range:** 50 to 85 kilometers (**31 to 53 miles**)
- **Temperature:** Decreases with altitude, reaching the coldest temperatures in the atmosphere, as low as -90°C
- **Composition:** Contains very thin air with very few molecules

Significance for Aviation

The mesosphere is less significant for conventional aviation due to its altitude, which is beyond the reach of commercial and military aircraft. However, it is of interest for aerospace operations and research. This layer is also where most meteoroids burn up upon entering the Earth's atmosphere, creating shooting stars.

4. Thermosphere

Characteristics

- **Altitude Range:** 85 to 600 kilometers (**53 to 373 miles**)
- **Temperature:** Increases significantly with altitude, can rise above 2,500°C
- **Composition:** Contains a small fraction of the atmosphere's mass, with molecules spread far apart

Significance for Aviation

The thermosphere is home to the International Space Station (**ISS**) and many low Earth orbit (**LEO**) satellites. While conventional aircraft cannot reach this layer, understanding the thermosphere is essential for space missions and satellite operations. The high temperatures in this layer are due to the absorption of highly energetic solar radiation.

5. Exosphere

Characteristics

- **Altitude Range:** 600 kilometers to 10,000 kilometers (**373 to 6,200 miles**)
- **Temperature:** Can be extremely high, but temperature is not felt the same way due to low density
- **Composition:** Consists mainly of hydrogen and helium atoms, with particles so sparse that they can travel hundreds of kilometers without colliding

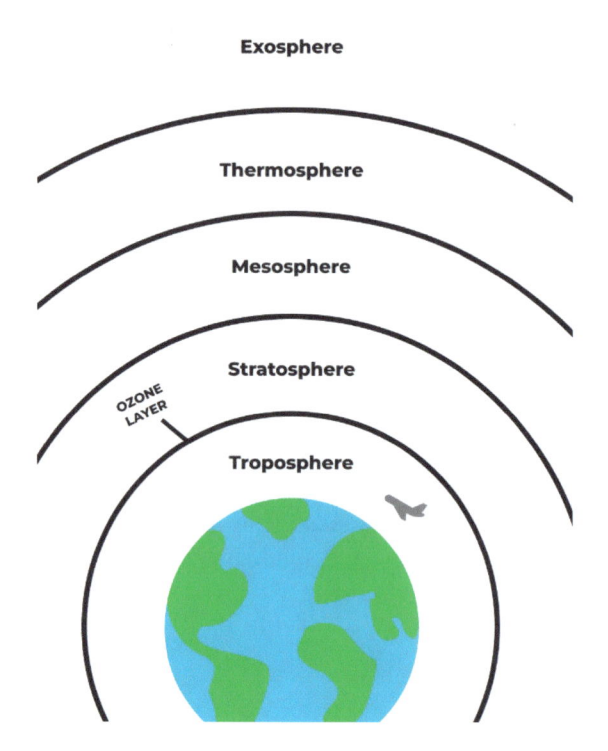

Significance for Aviation

The exosphere is the outermost layer of the Earth's atmosphere, gradually transitioning into outer space. While it is beyond the realm of traditional aviation, the exosphere is important for understanding the behavior of particles that escape into space and for the planning of deep-space missions.

Weather Fronts

Weather fronts are critical features in meteorology that have significant implications for aviation. A front represents the boundary between two distinct air masses with different temperatures, humidity levels, and densities. Understanding weather fronts is essential for pilots to navigate through different weather conditions safely. This chapter explores the types of weather fronts, their characteristics, and their impact on aviation.

Types of Weather Fronts

Weather fronts are generally classified into four main types: cold fronts, warm fronts, stationary fronts, and occluded fronts. Each type has unique features and weather patterns associated with it.

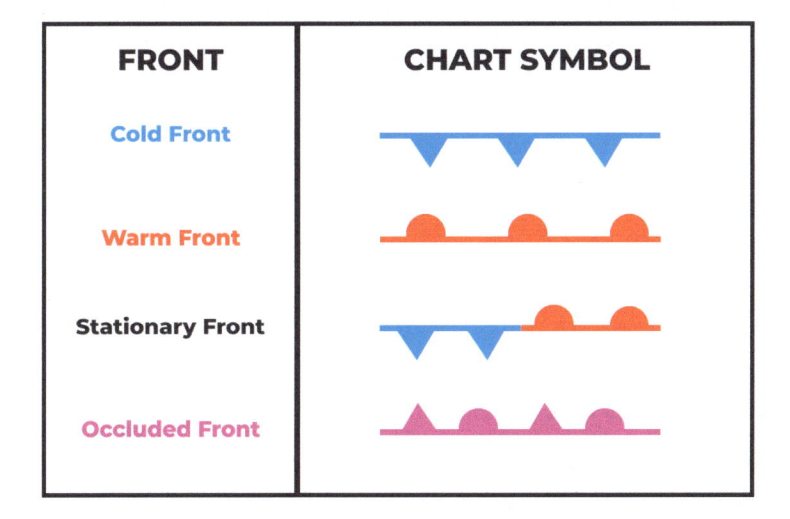

FRONT	CHART SYMBOL
Cold Front	▼▼▼
Warm Front	⏶⏶⏶
Stationary Front	▼ ⏶⏶
Occluded Front	▲⏶▲⏶

Cold Front

Characteristics:

- **Formation:** A cold front forms when a cold air mass pushes into a warmer air mass. Cold fronts move rapidly, often twice as fast as warm fronts.

- **Weather Patterns:** As the cold air, being denser, pushes under the lighter warm air, the warm air is lifted into the troposphere. This process leads to the formation of cumulus or cumulonimbus clouds, often resulting in thunderstorms. As the front passes, expect gusty winds, a sharp temperature drop, and heavy rain, possibly accompanied by hail, thunder, and lightning. Atmospheric pressure also shifts from falling to rising.

Impact on Aviation:

Cold fronts can cause significant turbulence and severe weather, posing challenges for flight operations. Pilots need to be vigilant about wind shear and turbulence ahead of cold fronts and plan for potential diversions or delays due to adverse weather.

Cold Front

Warm Front

Characteristics:

- Formation: A warm front forms when a warm air mass moves into a cooler air mass. These fronts typically move more slowly than cold fronts.

- Weather Patterns: The warm air rises over the cooler air, leading to cloud formation and steady precipitation. Ahead of a warm front, high clouds like cirrus and cirrostratus appear, followed by middle clouds like altostratus. Rain or snow is common as the front passes, with potential thunderstorms if the air is unstable.

Impact on Aviation:

Warm fronts bring extensive cloud cover and steady precipitation, reducing visibility and potentially causing icing conditions. Pilots should be prepared for instrument flight rules (**IFR**) conditions and monitor for ice accumulation on aircraft surfaces.

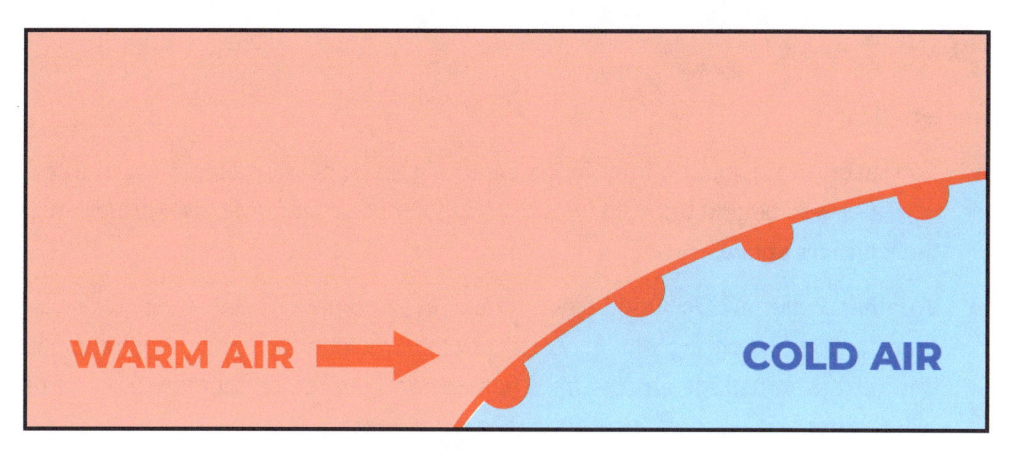

Warm Front

Stationary Front

Characteristics:

- Formation: A stationary front occurs when a cold front or warm front stops moving. This happens when two air masses are pushing against each other without one being strong enough to move the other.

- Weather Patterns: Stationary fronts can stay in place for days, leading to prolonged cloudiness and precipitation. The weather can vary along the front, with differences in temperature and wind on opposite sides.

Impact on Aviation:

Stationary fronts can cause extended periods of adverse weather, leading to low visibility and potential flight delays. Pilots need to continuously monitor weather conditions and be prepared for potential changes in flight plans.

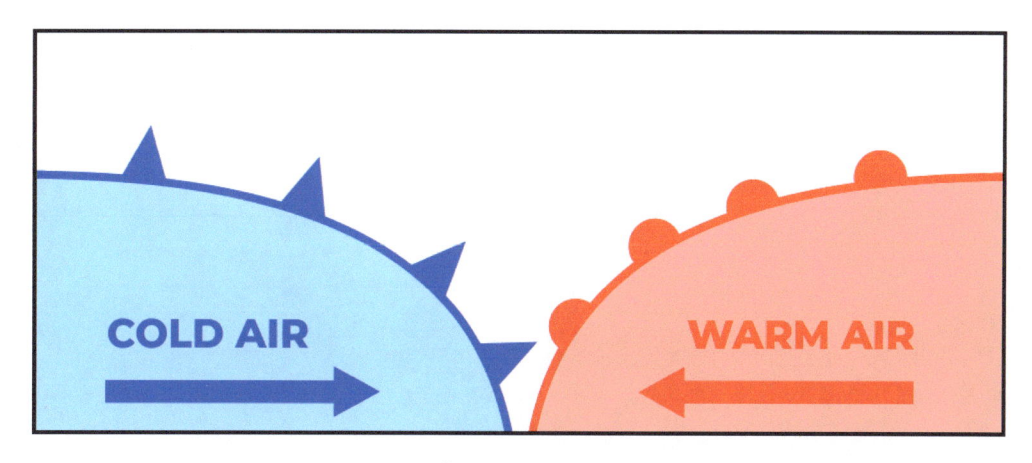

Stationary Front

Meteorology for Aviators | 145

Occluded Front

Characteristics:

- Formation: An occluded front forms when a cold front overtakes a warm front. The cold air mass behind the cold front meets the cool air ahead of the warm front, lifting the warm air above.

- Weather Patterns: Occluded fronts often bring complex weather, including heavy precipitation and strong winds, typically from cumulonimbus or nimbostratus clouds. Wind direction changes as the front passes, and the temperature may either rise or fall. Clearer skies and drier air often follow the front's passage.

Impact on Aviation:

Occluded fronts present challenging flying conditions due to the combination of cold and warm front weather patterns. Pilots must be cautious of severe weather and continuously monitor updates to ensure safe navigation.

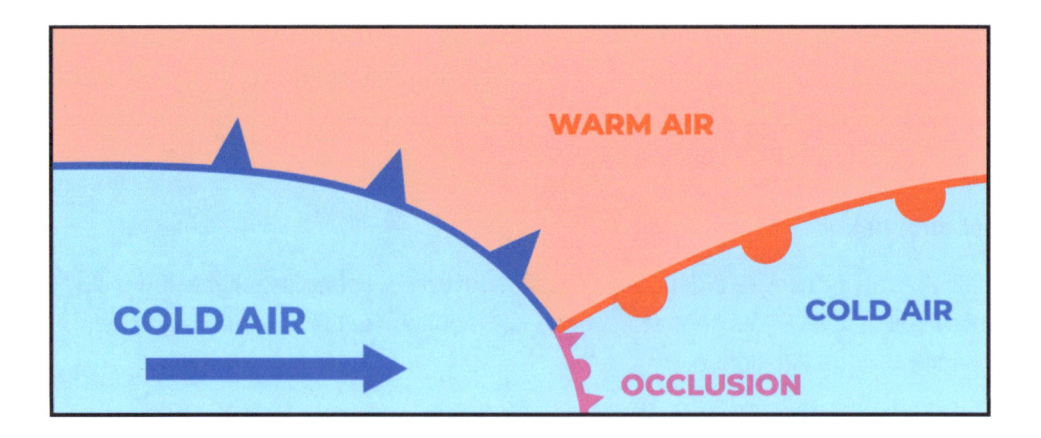

Understanding Weather Charts, NOTAMs, and TAFs

Weather plays a critical role in aviation, influencing everything from flight planning to in-flight decision-making. Pilots must have a solid understanding of weather forecasts and other crucial information before taking off. This chapter will cover three essential elements that pilots use to gather and interpret weather data: weather charts, NOTAMs, and TAFs.

Weather Charts

Weather charts provide visual information about weather patterns, including pressure systems, fronts, and areas of precipitation. They are an essential tool for understanding the overall weather picture along a flight route. Some key weather charts include:

Surface Analysis Chart

- Shows pressure systems (**highs and lows**), fronts (**cold, warm, stationary**), and precipitation areas.
- Helps pilots identify areas of turbulence, cloud cover, and potential storms.

Significant Weather Prognostic Chart

- Indicates potential areas of turbulence, icing, and significant weather phenomena (**e.g., thunderstorms, fog**).
- Helps pilots plan routes to avoid hazardous weather.

Winds and Temperature Aloft Chart

- Provides information on wind direction, speed, and temperatures at different altitudes.
- Essential for fuel planning and determining optimal cruising altitude.

NOTAMs (Notice to Airmen)

NOTAMs are essential messages that provide timely information about hazards, airport closures, or other unusual conditions that could affect a flight. They may include:

Airfield Closures or Restrictions

- Temporary runway closures, taxiway construction, or restricted airspace areas.
- Pilots must review these to ensure their destination or alternate airports are operational.

Navigation Aid Outages

- Information on inoperative or malfunctioning navigation aids (**like VORs, ILS systems**).
- Important for pilots relying on specific navigation equipment during their flight.

Temporary Airspace Restrictions

- Includes events like airshows, military exercises, or emergency operations.
- Pilots must avoid these areas or be prepared to follow ATC instructions.

```
A1234/24 NOTAMR A5678/23
Q) EGLL/QMRLC/IV/NBO/A/000/999/5129N00028W005
A) EGLL
B) 2408051200 C) 2408051800
E) RWY 09R/27L CLOSED DUE TO MAINTENANCE
```

NOTAM

A1234/24 NOTAMR A5678/23

Q) EGLL/QMRLC/IV/NBO/A/000/999/5129N00028W005

A) EGLL

B) 2408051200 C) 2408051800

E) RWY 09R/27L CLOSED DUE TO MAINTENANCE

Explanation:

- **A1234/24:** Unique identifier for this NOTAM, indicating it was issued in 2024.
- **NOTAMR A5678/23:** Replaces NOTAM A5678 from 2023.
- Q) EGLL/QMRLC/IV/NBO/A/000/999/5129N00028W005:
- Q): Code group detailing affected area and type of notice (**Runway closure**).
    - **EGLL:** ICAO code for Heathrow Airport.
    - **QMRLC:** Runway closure classification code.
    - **IV/NBO/A:** Scope and purpose of the NOTAM.
    - **000/999:** From ground level to unlimited altitude.
    - **5129N00028W005:** Coordinates and radius affected.
- A) **EGLL:** Location (**Heathrow Airport**).
- B) **2408051200:** Start time (**August 5, 2024, at 12:00 UTC**).
- C) **2408051800:** End time (**August 5, 2024, at 18:00 UTC**).
- E) RWY 09R/27L CLOSED DUE TO MAINTENANCE: Description—runway 09R/27L is closed for maintenance.

This NOTAM notifies pilots that a major runway at Heathrow will be temporarily closed, which is crucial for planning departures, arrivals, and diversions.

TAFs (Terminal Aerodrome Forecasts)

TAFs provide detailed weather forecasts for specific airports, usually within a 5-nautical-mile radius. These forecasts are updated regularly (**typically every 6 hours**) and cover a 24- to 30-hour period. A TAF includes:

Wind Speed and Direction

- Helps pilots understand the expected wind conditions during takeoff, en route, and landing.
- Allows for better planning of runway use and fuel consumption.

Visibility and Weather Conditions

- Indicates visibility in the area and any adverse weather conditions like fog, rain, snow, or thunderstorms.
- Critical for determining whether VFR (**Visual Flight Rules**) or IFR (**Instrument Flight Rules**) conditions will apply.

Cloud Cover

- Provides information on cloud layers, their altitudes, and coverage (**scattered, broken, overcast**).
- Important for determining if the flight can be conducted under visual flight rules or requires instrument flying.

```
TAF KJFK 121730Z 1218/1318 25015G25KT P6SM SCT030 BKN080
TEMPO 1220/1224 4SM -SHRA BKN015
FM130000 27012KT P6SM OVC020
TEMPO 1302/1306 3SM -SHSN OVC012
FM130800 30018G30KT P6SM SCT020 OVC050
TEMPO 1310/1314 2SM -SN BKN008
FM131500 32020G35KT P6SM BKN020
```

TAF

TAF KJFK 121730Z 1218/1318 25015G25KT P6SM SCT030 BKN080

   TEMPO 1220/1224 4SM -SHRA BKN015

   FM130000 27012KT P6SM OVC020

   TEMPO 1302/1306 3SM -SHSN OVC012

   FM130800 30018G30KT P6SM SCT020 OVC050

   TEMPO 1310/1314 2SM -SN BKN008

   FM131500 32020G35KT P6SM BKN020

Explanation

- **TAF KJFK:** Forecast for JFK Airport.
- **121730Z:** Issued on the 12th at 1730 UTC.
- **1218/1318:** Valid from 1800 UTC on the 12th to 1800 UTC on the 13th.

1. **25015G25KT P6SM SCT030 BKN080:** Wind from 250° at 15 knots, gusting to 25 knots; visibility over 6 miles; scattered clouds at 3,000 ft, broken clouds at 8,000 ft.
2. **TEMPO 1220/1224 4SM -SHRA BKN015:** Temporary drop to 4 miles visibility with light rain showers and broken clouds at 1,500 ft between 2000-2400 UTC.
3. **FM130000 27012KT P6SM OVC020:** From midnight, wind from 270° at 12 knots; overcast clouds at 2,000 ft.
4. **TEMPO 1302/1306 3SM -SHSN OVC012:** Brief periods of light snow showers with 3 miles visibility and overcast clouds at 1,200 ft.
5. **FM130800 30018G30KT P6SM SCT020 OVC050:** Wind from 300° at 18 knots, gusting to 30 knots; scattered clouds at 2,000 ft, overcast at 5,000 ft.
6. **FM131500 32020G35KT P6SM BKN020:** Stronger winds from 320° at 20 knots, gusting to 35 knots; broken clouds at 2,000 ft.

This summary captures the essential details pilots need for pre-flight planning, highlighting wind, visibility, and cloud conditions.

METAR

A METAR is an aviation routine weather report that provides critical weather information for pilots, meteorologists, and air traffic controllers. These reports are issued at regular intervals, typically once an hour, or more frequently in case of significant weather changes. METAR reports are standardized by the International Civil Aviation Organization (ICAO) and are used globally to provide real-time weather conditions at airports.

METAR Structure and Elements

A typical METAR report contains several components that describe the current weather conditions. The format is highly structured, consisting of the following elements:

EDDM 221620Z 27015KT 9999 SCT020 18/12 Q1018 NOSIG

Report Type

METAR: Routine weather report.

SPECI: A special weather report issued when significant weather changes occur between routine reports.

Station Identifier

A four-letter ICAO code that identifies the reporting station

(usually an airport). For example:

- EDDF for Frankfurt Airport.
- KJFK for John F. Kennedy International Airport.

Date and Time

The report includes the date and time of observation in UTC (Coordinated Universal Time). For example, 121350Z means the 12th day of the month at 13:50 UTC.

Wind

Wind speed and direction are reported in degrees and knots. For example:

- 24010KT means wind from 240° at 10 knots.
- If gusts are present, they are also included (e.g., 24010G18KT indicates gusts up to 18 knots).

Visibility

Reported in meters or statute miles, visibility indicates the distance a pilot can see:

- 9999 means visibility of 10 kilometers or more.
- 8000 means visibility of 8 kilometers.
- If less than 1,600 meters, visibility is given in meters (e.g., 1200).

Meteorology for Aviators | 153

Weather Phenomena

Present weather conditions are coded using abbreviations. Some common examples include:

- RA for rain,
- SN for snow,
- FG for fog,
- TS for thunderstorms.

Modifiers can further describe intensity or proximity, such as:

- -RA for light rain,
- +SN for heavy snow.

Sky Conditions

The amount and type of cloud cover are described in octas (eighths of the sky covered):

- FEW for 1-2 octas,
- SCT for scattered (**3-4 octas**),
- BKN for broken (**5-7 octas**),
- OVC for overcast (**8 octas**). Cloud heights are reported in hundreds of feet above ground level (**AGL**), e.g., BKN020 means broken clouds at 2,000 feet AGL.

Temperature and Dew Point

Temperature and dew point are reported in degrees Celsius. For example:

- 15/09 indicates a temperature of 15°C and a dew point of 9°C.
- A temperature-dew point spread that is close together may indicate fog or mist.

Altimeter (Pressure)

Atmospheric pressure is reported in hectopascals (**hPa**) or inches of mercury (**inHg**). For example:

- Q1013 means 1013 hPa,
- A2992 means 29.92 inHg.

Remarks (RMK)

Additional information can be included in the RMK section, such as runway conditions, wind shear, or automated observations.

Example METAR

> **METAR EDDF 121350Z 24010KT 9999 SCT025 15/09 Q1013 NOSIG**

EDDF: Frankfurt Airport.

121350Z: Report issued on the 12th day at 13:50 UTC.

24010KT: Wind from 240° at 10 knots.

9999: Visibility 10 km or more.

SCT025: Scattered clouds at 2,500 feet.

15/09: Temperature 15°C, dew point 9°C.

Q1013: Pressure is 1013 hPa.

NOSIG: No significant changes expected in the near future.

METARs are essential tools for flight planning and operations. Pilots use these reports to assess current weather conditions at the departure and arrival airports, as well as along the flight path. For example, high winds, low visibility, or storm activity might require flight adjustments, such as changing altitudes or delaying takeoff. METARs also play a role in flight safety, helping pilots avoid dangerous weather phenomena like thunderstorms, icing conditions, or wind shear.

Chapter 7

Air Traffic Control and Communication

ATC

Air Traffic Control (**ATC**) is a crucial component of aviation, ensuring the safe and efficient movement of aircraft in the skies and on the ground. This chapter delves into the functions, responsibilities, and importance of ATC in the aviation industry.

What is Air Traffic Control (ATC)?

Air Traffic Control is a service provided by ground-based controllers who coordinate the movement of aircraft both in the air and on the ground. These controllers work to prevent collisions, organize and expedite the flow of air traffic, and provide information and support for pilots.

Functions of ATC:

En-Route Control

En-route controllers manage aircraft flying at higher altitudes in controlled airspace between airports. They ensure that aircraft maintain safe distances from each other, usually by using radar and communication systems.

Terminal Control

Terminal controllers handle aircraft in the vicinity of an airport. They guide aircraft during the critical phases of departure and arrival, ensuring safe sequencing and spacing.

Ground Control

Ground controllers manage all aircraft and vehicular movement on the airport's taxiways and runways. They coordinate the movement of aircraft from parking stands to the runway and vice versa, ensuring safe and orderly flow.

Tower Control

Tower controllers oversee aircraft takeoffs and landings. They are responsible for granting clearances for aircraft to land or take off and ensuring that the runway is clear of any obstacles or other aircraft.

Roles and Responsibilities:

Preventing Collisions

The primary responsibility of ATC is to prevent collisions between aircraft. This is achieved through maintaining safe separation distances, providing clear instructions to pilots, and constantly monitoring aircraft positions.

Expediting Traffic Flow

ATC ensures that air traffic flows smoothly and efficiently. By managing flight paths, altitudes, and speeds, controllers help to reduce delays and optimize the use of airspace.

Providing Information and Assistance

Controllers provide pilots with vital information, such as weather updates, navigational aid, and information about other aircraft. They also assist in emergency situations, offering guidance and support to ensure a safe outcome.

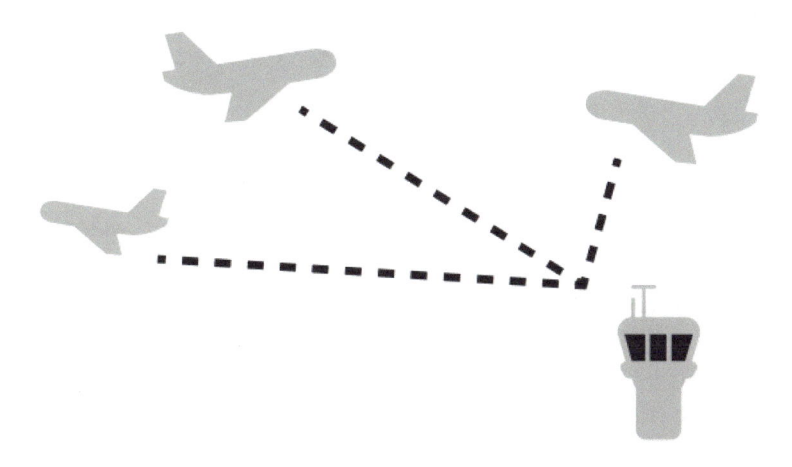

The ATC System:

Radar and Communication

Radar systems are essential for ATC operations, allowing controllers to track aircraft positions and movements accurately. Communication between ATC and pilots is conducted via radio frequencies, ensuring clear and precise instructions are relayed.

Air Traffic Control Centers

ATC services are provided from various control centers, including Area Control Centers (**ACC**) for en-route traffic, Approach Control Facilities for terminal areas, and Control Towers at airports. Each center plays a specific role in managing different phases of flight.

Standard Operating Procedures (SOPs)

ATC operations follow strict SOPs to ensure safety and consistency. These procedures dictate how controllers should handle various situations, from routine operations to emergencies.

Challenges in ATC:

High Traffic Volume

Managing a large volume of air traffic, especially during peak times, can be challenging. Controllers must be vigilant and efficient to prevent congestion and ensure safety.

Weather Conditions

Adverse weather conditions, such as thunderstorms, fog, and high winds, pose significant challenges for ATC. Controllers must provide timely and accurate information to pilots and make adjustments to flight paths as necessary.

Human Factors

The human element in ATC is critical, as controllers must make quick decisions under pressure. Fatigue, stress, and communication errors can impact performance, highlighting the need for robust training and support systems.

Air Traffic Control is a vital element of aviation, ensuring that aircraft operate safely and efficiently. The complex and demanding nature of ATC requires skilled controllers who can manage a dynamic and sometimes unpredictable environment. Through advanced technology, stringent procedures, and dedicated professionals, ATC continues to play a key role in the safety and success of the aviation industry.

VFR & IFR

In aviation, pilots operate under two primary sets of regulations: Visual Flight Rules (**VFR**) and Instrument Flight Rules (**IFR**). These rules dictate the conditions under which a pilot may operate an aircraft, including weather minimums, navigation methods, and required training. Understanding the differences between VFR and IFR is crucial for pilots and aviation enthusiasts alike, as it impacts flight planning, safety, and overall flight operations.

Visual Flight Rules (VFR):

Definition and Purpose

Visual Flight Rules refer to the set of regulations under which a pilot operates an aircraft in weather conditions generally clear enough to allow the pilot to see where the aircraft is going. The primary purpose of VFR is to ensure pilots maintain visual reference to the ground, other aircraft, and obstacles to navigate and avoid collisions.

Weather Requirements

VFR operations require specific weather conditions known as Visual Meteorological Conditions (**VMC**). These conditions typically include minimum visibility and distance from clouds, which vary depending on the airspace and altitude. For instance, in controlled airspace, VMC might require a visibility of at least three miles and cloud clearance of 500 feet below, 1,000 feet above, and 2,000 feet horizontally.

Navigation

Under VFR, pilots primarily navigate using visual references such as landmarks, roads, rivers, and other features on the ground. Pilots may also use basic navigation aids like VOR (**VHF Omnidirectional Range**) and GPS to supplement their visual navigation.

Training and Certification

To operate under VFR, pilots must obtain a private pilot license (**PPL**) or higher. Training focuses on visual navigation, weather interpretation, and collision avoidance techniques.

Limitations

VFR flight is limited to conditions where visibility is adequate for safe navigation. It is not suitable for flying in clouds, heavy rain, fog, or other conditions that reduce visibility. Additionally, VFR is typically restricted to daytime operations, though night VFR is allowed under specific conditions and with additional training.

Instrument Flight Rules (IFR):

Definition and Purpose

Instrument Flight Rules refer to the regulations under which a pilot operates an aircraft in weather conditions that do not meet VFR minimums, such as low visibility or cloud cover. IFR enables pilots to fly in a wider range of weather conditions by relying on instruments for navigation and aircraft control.

Weather Requirements

IFR operations are designed for conditions known as Instrument Meteorological Conditions (**IMC**), where visibility is poor, and pilots cannot rely on visual references. IFR flight is allowed in both VMC and IMC, providing greater flexibility for flight planning and operations.

Navigation

Under IFR, pilots navigate using a suite of instruments and avionics, including the flight management system (**FMS**), VOR, NDB (**Non-Directional Beacon**), DME (**Distance Measuring Equipment**), and GPS. These tools allow precise navigation and ensure the aircraft remains on its intended flight path.

Training and Certification

Pilots must obtain an instrument rating (**IR**) in addition to their private or commercial pilot license to operate under IFR. This advanced training includes mastering the use of navigation instruments, understanding instrument approach procedures, and flying without outside visual references.

Air Traffic Control (ATC)

IFR flights are closely managed by air traffic control (**ATC**). Pilots must file an IFR flight plan and receive clearances for routes, altitudes, and approaches. ATC provides separation services, ensuring safe distances between aircraft in controlled airspace.

Limitations

While IFR allows flight in a wider range of weather conditions, it requires rigorous adherence to procedures and reliance on instruments. It demands high levels of skill and concentration, especially in challenging conditions like thunderstorms or severe turbulence.

Comparison of VFR and IFR:

Visibility Requirements

- **VFR:** Requires clear weather and good visibility.
- **IFR:** Allows flight in poor visibility and adverse weather conditions.

Navigation

- **VFR:** Primarily visual navigation using landmarks.
- **IFR:** Instrument-based navigation using avionics.

Training

- **VFR:** Requires a private pilot license.
- **IFR:** Requires an instrument rating in addition to a pilot license.

ATC Interaction

- **VFR:** Limited ATC interaction, mainly for controlled airspace.
- **IFR:** Continuous ATC communication and clearances required.

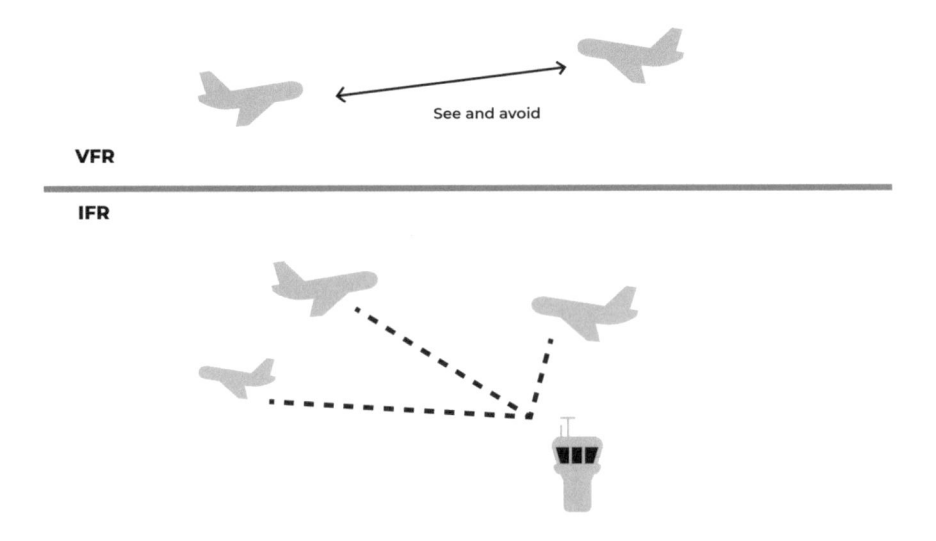

Phraseology and Communication

Effective communication is a cornerstone of safe and efficient flight operations. In aviation, clear, concise, and standardized language, known as phraseology, is used to minimize misunderstandings and ensure that instructions are understood correctly. The International Civil Aviation Organization (**ICAO**) mandates specific terms and phrases to be used in communication between pilots and air traffic control (**ATC**) worldwide. Understanding and following these communication protocols is essential for pilots at every stage of flight.

Importance of Standardized Phraseology

Using standardized phraseology ensures that all parties involved in air traffic operations understand the same language, regardless of their native language or region. Ambiguous or unclear communication can lead to dangerous situations, such as runway incursions, altitude deviations, or incorrect heading assignments. Standard phraseology helps eliminate these risks by establishing common and universally understood terms.

Key principles of effective communication include:

- **Brevity:** Keep transmissions as short and clear as possible.
- **Clarity:** Speak slowly, enunciate clearly, and avoid unnecessary words.
- **Accuracy:** Use correct terms and repeat critical information to confirm understanding.

Basic ATC Communication Structure

The general structure of ATC communication follows a predictable pattern to ensure consistency:

1. **Identification:** Both the pilot and ATC will begin by identifying themselves. The pilot uses the aircraft call sign (**e.g., "Delta 123"**) and ATC uses the station identifier (**e.g., "Frankfurt Ground"**).
2. **Message:** The main content of the message is conveyed, such as taxi instructions, altitude assignments, or heading changes.
3. **Acknowledgment:** The recipient of the message (**either the pilot or ATC**) repeats back the key parts of the message to confirm understanding. This is known as a readback.
4. **Confirmation:** The message is confirmed, and both parties know that the instruction has been received correctly.

Example:

- **ATC:** "Frankfurt Tower, Lufthansa 456, cleared for takeoff runway 25R."
- **Pilot:** "Cleared for takeoff runway 25R, Lufthansa 456."

Air Traffic Control and Communication | 165

Commonly Used ATC Phrases

Here are some of the most commonly used phrases in ATC communication:

Takeoff and Landing

- **Cleared for takeoff:** The aircraft is given permission to take off.
- **Cleared to land:** The aircraft is given permission to land on a specific runway.
- **Hold short:** Instructs the aircraft to stop before reaching a specific point, such as a runway.
- **Line up and wait:** Instructs the aircraft to enter the runway and wait for further clearance.

Altitude and Heading Instructions

Climb and maintain: Instructs the aircraft to climb to a specified altitude and maintain that altitude (**e.g., "Climb and maintain 10,000 feet"**).

Descend and maintain: Instructs the aircraft to descend to a specific altitude.

Fly heading: ATC assigns a specific compass heading for the aircraft to follow.

Airspace and Traffic

Traffic in sight: The pilot confirms that they have visual contact with other aircraft in the area.

Radar contact: ATC confirms that the aircraft is identified on radar.

Clear of conflict: ATC informs the pilot that potential conflicts with other aircraft have been resolved.

Weather and Turbulence

Request vectors for weather: The pilot requests a deviation from the planned route to avoid bad weather.

Report turbulence: ATC asks the pilot to report turbulence levels.

Light/Moderate/Severe turbulence: Pilots report the intensity of turbulence encountered.

The Phonetic Alphabet

Aviation uses the NATO phonetic alphabet to spell out letters clearly, especially when transmitting call signs, runway numbers, or locations. This ensures that letters are not confused, even in noisy environments or during poor radio transmissions.

A	Alpha	L	Lima	W	Whiskey
B	Bravo	M	Mike	X	X-Ray
C	Charlie	N	November	Y	Yankee
D	Delta	O	Oscar	Z	Zulu
E	Echo	P	Papa		
F	Foxtrot	Q	Quebec		
G	Golf	R	Romeo		
H	Hotel	S	Sierra		
I	India	T	Tango		
J	Juliet	U	Uniform		
K	Kilo	V	Victor		

Example:

Call sign "DL123" would be transmitted as "Delta Lima One Two Three".

Readbacks and Hearbacks

The readback/hearback process is one of the most important safety measures in ATC communication. When ATC gives instructions, the pilot is required to read back key parts of the message, such as the assigned altitude, heading, or clearance. ATC then performs a hearback check to ensure that the message was correctly understood.

This process helps prevent misunderstandings and ensures that both the pilot and ATC are aligned in their actions.

Air Traffic Control and Communication | 167

Example:

- **ATC:** "American 452, descend and maintain 5,000 feet."
- **Pilot:** "Descend and maintain 5,000 feet, American 452."
- **ATC:** "American 452, correct."

Best Practices for Effective Communication

Here are some best practices for both pilots and ATC when communicating:

- **Listen first:** Always wait for a break in communication before transmitting.
- **Be concise:** Only include necessary information, and avoid over-explaining.
- **Use standard phraseology:** Always use ICAO-approved terminology to avoid confusion.
- **Prioritize clarity:** Speak at a moderate pace, and ensure every word is clear.
- **Avoid assumptions:** Never assume instructions have been correctly received without confirmation.
- **Ask for clarification:** If unsure about an instruction, request clarification instead of guessing.

Common Terms:

- **Say again:** Used to ask for a repeat of the previous transmission.
- **Unable:** Indicates that a request cannot be complied with (**e.g., due to aircraft performance or safety**).
- **Stand by:** Tells the other party to wait for further information

Understanding Airspace Classes

As a private pilot, understanding airspace classes is essential for safe navigation and compliance with aviation regulations. Airspace is categorized into several classes, each with specific rules, requirements, and operational procedures. This chapter will explore the different airspace classes, their characteristics, and how they affect flight operations.

Overview of Airspace Classes

Airspace in the United States is divided into several classes, primarily designated as Class **A, B, C, D, E, and G**. Each class has distinct operational rules, visibility requirements, and aircraft equipment requirements.

Class A Airspace

Altitude: From 18,000 feet MSL (**Mean Sea Level**) to FL600 (**Flight Level 600**).

Requirements:

- IFR (**Instrument Flight Rules**) only.
- ATC clearance required for entry.
- All aircraft must be equipped with a transponder and ADS-B (Automatic Dependent Surveillance–Broadcast).

Characteristics: This is the highest level of controlled airspace, where all flights must be under the direction of Air Traffic Control (**ATC**). VFR flights are not permitted.

Class B Airspace

Altitude: Typically from the surface to 10,000 feet MSL, surrounding major airports.

Requirements:

- ATC clearance required for entry.
- Must have a two-way radio communication capability.
- Must be equipped with a transponder.

Characteristics: Class B airspace is designed to protect high-traffic areas around busy airports. Pilots must receive clearance from ATC before entering this airspace. VFR pilots need to have specific visibility and cloud clearance requirements.

Class C Airspace

Altitude: Typically from the surface to 4,000 feet above the airport elevation, with a radius of about 5 nautical miles.

Requirements:

- ATC communication is required, but not a specific clearance.
- Must have a transponder.

Characteristics: Class C airspace surrounds airports with a significant level of traffic. Pilots must establish radio contact with ATC before entering this airspace. There are no specific VFR clearance requirements, but pilots must comply with visibility and cloud clearance rules.

Class D Airspace

Altitude: Generally extends from the surface to 2,500 feet above the airport elevation.

Requirements:

- ATC communication required.
- No transponder requirement, but it may be needed based on the surrounding airspace.

Characteristics: Class D airspace surrounds airports with control towers. Pilots must establish communication with the tower before entering. VFR weather minimums apply.

Class E Airspace

Altitude: Can begin at various altitudes, usually starting at 1,200 feet AGL (**Above Ground Level**) or higher, but may also extend from the surface in certain locations.

Requirements:

- No ATC clearance required, but communication is encouraged.

Characteristics: Class E airspace is considered controlled airspace but is not as restrictive as Classes A, B, C, or D. It is primarily used for IFR operations and can also include VFR flights. Visibility and cloud clearance requirements depend on the altitude and whether it's an IFR or VFR flight.

Class G Airspace

Altitude: Extends from the surface up to the base of the overlying Class E airspace.

Requirements:

- No ATC communication required.

Characteristics: Class G airspace is uncontrolled airspace. Pilots can operate without ATC clearance, but they must adhere to basic VFR weather minimums. This airspace is often found in rural areas and around small airports.

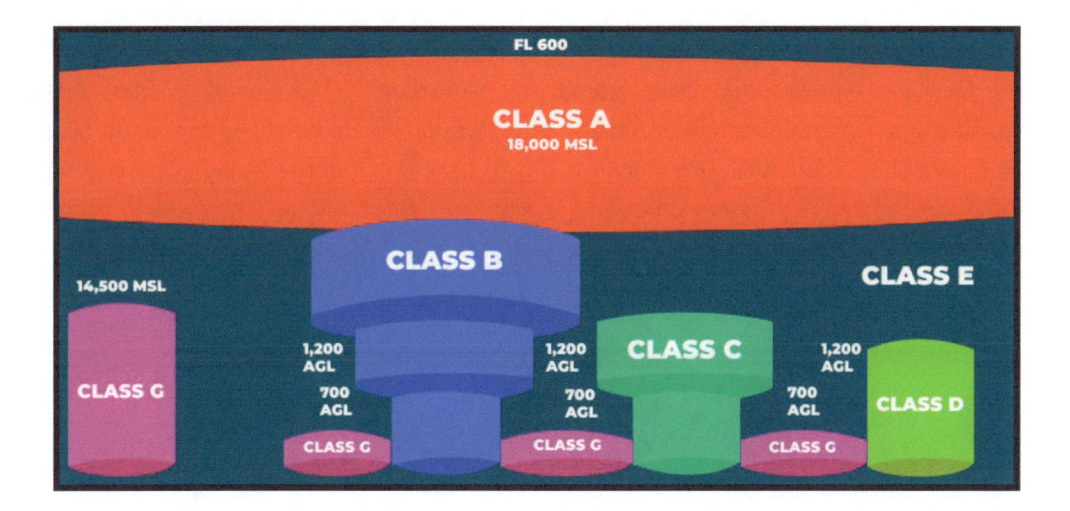

Understanding airspace classes is critical for the safety and efficiency of flight operations. As a private pilot, you must be familiar with the rules and requirements for each airspace class to navigate effectively and comply with regulations. Always ensure that you are aware of your position relative to airspace boundaries and communicate effectively with ATC when required.

By mastering the concepts presented in this chapter, you will enhance your situational awareness and improve your decision-making skills as a pilot.

TCAS - Traffic Collision Avoidance System

The skies are crowded with aircraft of various sizes and speeds, all navigating through the airspace with precision and caution. However, with such a dense and dynamic environment, the risk of mid-air collisions is ever-present. To mitigate this risk and ensure the safety of air travel, modern aircraft are equipped with advanced collision avoidance systems, with one of the most prominent being the Traffic Collision Avoidance System (**TCAS**). In this chapter, we will delve into the workings of TCAS, its components, modes of operation, and its crucial role in enhancing aviation safety.

Understanding TCAS:

Traffic Collision Avoidance System, commonly known as TCAS, is an avionics system designed to monitor the airspace around an aircraft and provide timely advisories to pilots to avoid potential collisions with other aircraft. TCAS operates independently of ground-based air traffic control and is primarily utilized to prevent mid-air collisions, especially in situations where aircraft are flying in close proximity to each other.

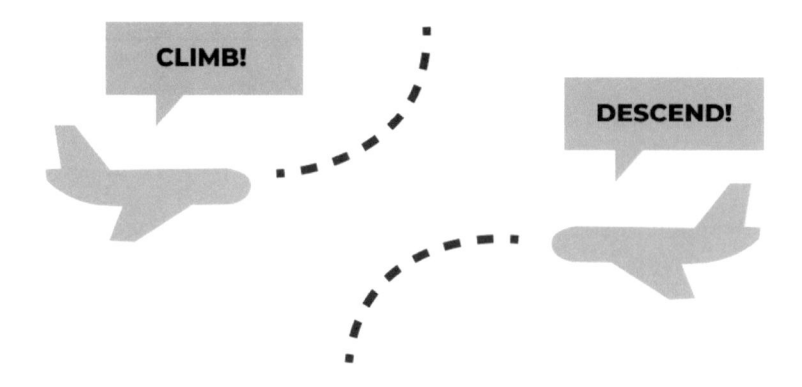

Components of TCAS:

Transponder

At the core of TCAS is the aircraft's transponder, which emits a unique identification code and altitude information to other aircraft and ground-based radar systems. The transponder plays a vital role in enabling TCAS to detect nearby aircraft and assess collision risks accurately.

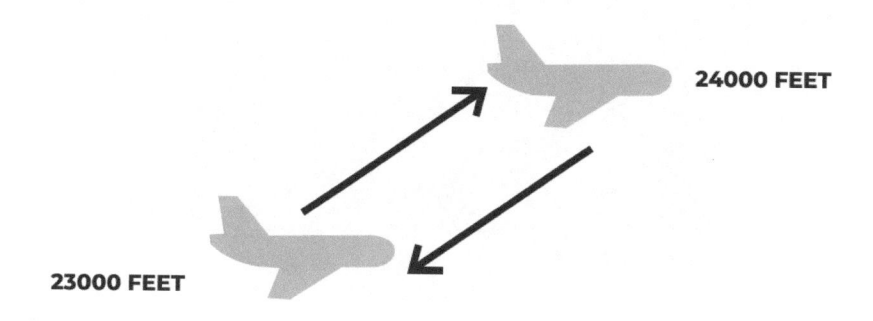

Antennas

TCAS antennas, typically located on the top and bottom of the aircraft fuselage, receive signals from nearby aircraft transponders. These antennas facilitate the detection and tracking of other aircraft within the vicinity.

Computing System

TCAS relies on a sophisticated computing system to analyze data from the transponder and antennas, assess the relative positions and trajectories of nearby aircraft, and generate collision avoidance advisories.

Modes of Operation:

Traffic Advisory (TA)

In the Traffic Advisory mode, TCAS provides pilots with visual and audible alerts regarding the presence of nearby aircraft that may pose a potential collision threat. These advisories prompt pilots to visually scan for the traffic and take evasive action if necessary.

Resolution Advisory (RA)

If TCAS determines that a potential collision is imminent, it issues Resolution Advisories to both pilots involved. These advisories include specific instructions for vertical maneuvering, such as climb or descent, to maintain safe separation from the conflicting aircraft.

Resolution Advisory (RA) Region

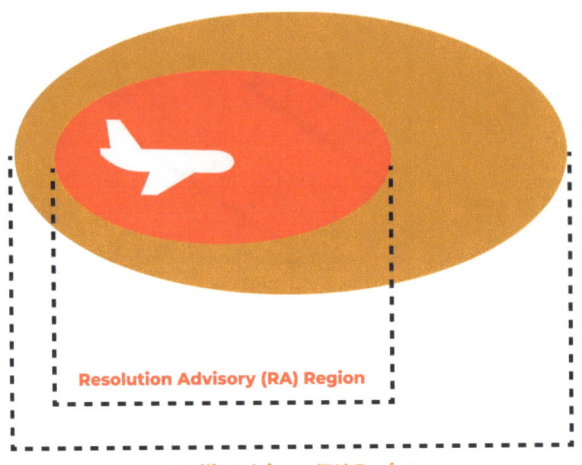

Traffic Advisory (TA) Region

Integration with Cockpit Displays:

TCAS advisories are typically displayed on the aircraft's cockpit display systems, allowing pilots to quickly assess the situation and respond accordingly. The TCAS display provides real-time information about the relative positions, altitudes, and trajectories of nearby aircraft, aiding pilots in making informed decisions to avoid collisions.

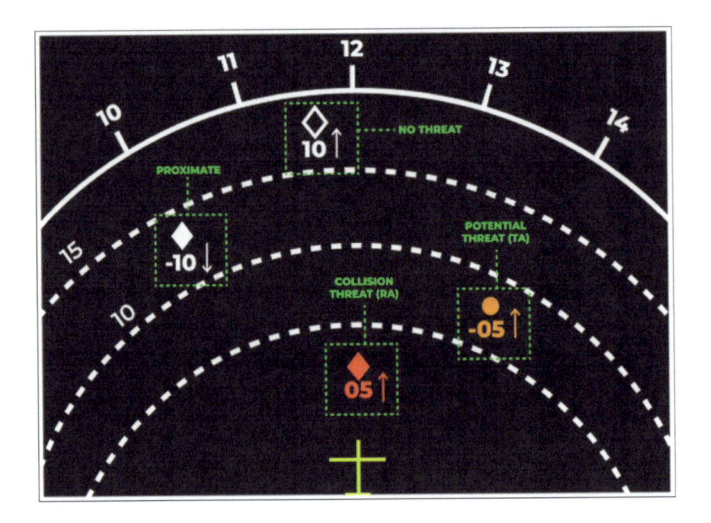

The Traffic Collision Avoidance System (**TCAS**) stands as a critical safety net in the modern airspace, helping pilots detect and avoid potential collisions with other aircraft. With its ability to operate independently of ground-based systems and provide timely advisories, TCAS enhances situational awareness and enables safe navigation through congested airspace, ultimately ensuring the continued safety and efficiency of air travel.

174 | Air Traffic Control and Communication

Chapter 8

Safety and Operational Procedures

The Importance of Pre-Flight Checklists

Before any aircraft takes to the skies, pilots follow a crucial routine: the pre-flight checklist. This is more than just a simple to-do list; it is a fundamental part of aviation safety.

Why Are Checklists Important?

Checklists ensure that pilots systematically verify the condition and functionality of the aircraft before each flight. They are designed to catch potential issues that might not be immediately obvious, from low oil levels to faulty instruments. Missing a single step could lead to serious safety risks, which is why strict adherence to these procedures is essential.

What's Included in a Pre-Flight Checklist?

A typical pre-flight checklist covers several areas of the aircraft, including:

- **Aircraft Documentation:** Ensuring that all required documents, like registration and airworthiness certificates, are on board.
- **External Inspection:** Checking the exterior of the aircraft for any visible damage, leaks, or obstructions. This includes inspecting the wings, fuselage, landing gear, and control surfaces.
- **Fuel and Oil Levels:** Verifying that there is sufficient fuel for the flight and that oil levels are within the required range.
- **Instruments and Avionics:** Testing the functionality of flight instruments, navigation systems, and communication equipment.
- **Flight Controls:** Ensuring that all control surfaces (**e.g., ailerons, elevators, rudders**) move freely and correctly.
- **Emergency Equipment:** Confirming that safety gear like life vests, fire extinguishers, and first aid kits are present and functional.

Checklists: A Safety Net Against Human Error

Flying is a complex task, and even the most experienced pilots can overlook details. That's where checklists serve as a safety net. By following a standardized procedure, pilots minimize the chances of missing something important. They also help in maintaining consistency, especially when operating different aircraft types.

Types of Checklists

There are different types of checklists depending on the phase of flight:

- **Pre-Flight:** Before the aircraft leaves the ground.
- **Taxi and Takeoff:** Final checks before takeoff to ensure everything is set for departure.
- **In-Flight:** Regular checks during flight to monitor systems.
- **Landing:** Preparations for landing, including configuring the aircraft for approach.
- **Shutdown and Post-Flight:** Securing the aircraft after landing.

The Role of Crew Resource Management (CRM)

Modern aviation emphasizes the use of Crew Resource Management (**CRM**) principles. This means that pilots are encouraged to work as a team, double-checking each other's actions and communicating openly. Checklists play a key role in CRM by providing a structured way for crews to verify that all critical tasks have been completed.

The pre-flight checklist is a small but mighty tool in aviation. It's a routine that has been perfected over decades and is key to ensuring the safety of every flight. Next time you see a pilot walking around the plane and ticking off items on a list, you'll know that they are following a strict procedure designed to keep everyone on board safe.

SOPs - Standard Operating Procedures

Standard Operating Procedures (**SOPs**) are essential in aviation for ensuring safety, efficiency, and consistency in operations. They provide a structured framework for pilots and crew to follow, reducing the likelihood of errors and enhancing overall operational performance. This chapter explores the importance, components, and implementation of SOPs in aviation.

Introduction to SOPs

SOPs are detailed, written instructions designed to achieve uniformity in the performance of specific functions. In aviation, SOPs cover all aspects of flight operations, from pre-flight preparations to post-flight procedures. They serve as a reference for best practices and ensure that all team members operate in harmony, adhering to the same protocols.

Importance of SOPs

The primary importance of SOPs lies in their ability to enhance safety. By providing clear guidelines on handling both normal and emergency situations, SOPs minimize risks. Consistency is another crucial benefit, as SOPs ensure that every flight operation is conducted in the same manner, regardless of who is performing the task. This uniformity helps prevent misunderstandings and errors. Efficiency is also improved through SOPs, as they streamline operations, reduce the time required for training, and enhance overall productivity. Furthermore, SOPs help in meeting regulatory requirements set by aviation authorities and organizations, ensuring compliance and standardization.

Importance of SOPs

SOPs in aviation typically encompass several critical elements:

- **Flying by Numbers:** This involves using predefined power settings, speeds, and altitudes to ensure consistent aircraft performance. By adhering to these standardized values, pilots can ensure that the aircraft operates within safe and efficient parameters, minimizing the risk of deviations and optimizing fuel consumption.

- **Flow Patterns:** These are sequences of actions performed by the crew to ensure all necessary tasks are completed methodically. Flow patterns help in organizing the cockpit tasks in a logical and efficient manner, ensuring that nothing is overlooked. They often follow a specific order, such as from left to right or top to bottom, to maintain consistency.

- **Checklists:** These are essential tools used to verify that all required steps are completed. Checklists serve as a double-check mechanism to ensure that no critical task is missed. They cover various phases of flight, including pre-flight, takeoff, in-flight, approach, landing, and post-flight, providing a structured approach to completing each phase safely.

- **Callouts:** These are verbal confirmations and announcements made by the crew to enhance communication and situational awareness. Callouts ensure that all crew members are aware of critical actions and changes in flight status, such as altitude changes, gear and flap positions, and other important flight parameters. This practice helps in maintaining a high level of coordination and reducing the likelihood of miscommunication.

- **Briefings:** These involve discussing important information and plans before and during the flight to ensure all crew members are on the same page. Briefings cover various aspects of the flight, including the flight plan, weather conditions, potential hazards, emergency procedures, and any other relevant information. Effective briefings help in preparing the crew for the flight and ensure that everyone is aware of their roles and responsibilities.

Developing SOPs

The development of SOPs involves several key steps. First, an assessment of current practices is conducted to identify areas that require standardization. This is followed by consultation with experienced pilots, crew members, and industry experts to gather insights and best practices. The documentation phase involves writing clear, concise, and comprehensive procedures, ensuring they are easily understood and followed. Once documented, SOPs must be regularly reviewed and updated to reflect changes in regulations, technology, and operational practices.

Implementing SOPs

Successful implementation of SOPs requires thorough training for all personnel, ensuring they understand and can execute the procedures. Continuous monitoring of adherence to SOPs is necessary, with feedback mechanisms in place to address deviations. Regular reinforcement through recurrent training and drills keeps SOPs top of mind. Additionally, periodic evaluation of SOP effectiveness is essential, making necessary adjustments based on feedback and operational experience.

Challenges in SOP Implementation

Implementing SOPs is not without its challenges. One significant challenge is overcoming resistance to change from personnel who may be accustomed to previous practices. Managing the complexity of developing SOPs that are comprehensive yet easy to follow is another hurdle. Ensuring consistent compliance with SOPs across all operations, especially in dynamic environments, can also be challenging.

Standard Operating Procedures are a cornerstone of safe and efficient aviation operations. They provide a structured approach to managing every aspect of flight, from routine tasks to emergency responses. By developing, implementing, and continuously improving SOPs, aviation organizations can enhance safety, ensure consistency, and achieve operational excellence. Regular training and reinforcement are crucial to maintaining the effectiveness of SOPs and ensuring that all personnel are equipped to perform their duties according to the highest standards. Incorporating elements such as flying by numbers, flow patterns, checklists, callouts, and briefings within SOPs further enhances their utility and effectiveness in promoting safe and efficient flight operations.

Crew Resource Management (CRM)

Crew Resource Management (**CRM**) is a crucial aspect of modern aviation, designed to enhance safety by improving teamwork, communication, decision-making, and situational awareness in the cockpit. CRM is not just about flying the aircraft; it's about managing all available resources—both human and technical—to ensure a safe and efficient flight. This chapter will explore the principles of CRM, its evolution, and its importance in aviation.

The Evolution of CRM

CRM was developed in response to a series of high-profile aviation accidents in the 1970s, where human error and poor communication were identified as contributing factors. Initially termed "*Cockpit Resource Management,*" the concept has since expanded beyond the cockpit to include all personnel involved in the flight, including cabin crew and ground staff. The term "*Crew Resource Management*" reflects this broader scope, emphasizing that safety is a shared responsibility.

The first formal CRM training programs were introduced in the late 1970s by airlines like United Airlines, following recommendations from the National Transportation Safety Board (**NTSB**) and NASA. These early programs focused on addressing the hierarchical nature of the cockpit, encouraging more open communication and collaboration among crew members. Over time, CRM has evolved to include various aspects of human factors, such as stress management, fatigue awareness, and decision-making under pressure.

Core Principles of CRM

CRM is built on several core principles that guide how crew members interact and make decisions during a flight. These principles are designed to mitigate the risks associated with human error, which remains one of the leading causes of aviation accidents.

- **Effective Communication:** Clear, concise, and assertive communication is essential in the cockpit. Pilots and crew must be able to express concerns, provide information, and ask questions without hesitation. CRM encourages a communication style where all crew members feel empowered to speak up if they notice something that could impact safety, regardless of rank or experience.

- **Teamwork:** Aviation is a team effort, and CRM emphasizes the importance of working together as a cohesive unit. This includes understanding each crew member's role and responsibilities, supporting one another, and being aware of each other's actions and intentions. Effective teamwork reduces the likelihood of errors and ensures that the crew can respond swiftly to any situation.

- **Decision-Making:** CRM promotes a structured approach to decision-making, where all available information is considered before taking action. This involves gathering input from all relevant sources, weighing the pros and cons of different options, and choosing the best course of action based on the situation. In critical situations, quick and decisive action is necessary, but CRM teaches pilots to balance urgency with thoroughness.

- **Situational Awareness:** Maintaining situational awareness means being aware of what is happening in and around the aircraft at all times. This includes monitoring the aircraft's systems, the external environment (such as weather and terrain), and the actions of other crew members. CRM training helps pilots develop the skills to stay focused and alert, even during long or complex flights, reducing the risk of errors caused by distractions or fatigue.

- **Workload Management:** Managing workload effectively is crucial for maintaining performance and safety, especially during high-stress situations such as takeoff, landing, or in-flight emergencies. CRM teaches pilots how to prioritize tasks, delegate responsibilities when necessary, and avoid becoming overloaded. Proper workload management helps ensure that critical tasks are completed accurately and on time, preventing mistakes that could compromise safety.

The Role of CRM in Preventing Accidents

One of the most significant impacts of CRM is its role in reducing the incidence of human error in aviation. Before CRM became widely adopted, many accidents were attributed to breakdowns in communication, poor decision-making, and a lack of coordination among crew members. By addressing these issues, CRM has significantly improved safety in the aviation industry.

For example, the *United Airlines Flight 232* accident in 1989 is often cited as a textbook case of effective CRM. Despite the catastrophic failure of the aircraft's hydraulic systems, which left the pilots with minimal control, the crew managed to work together, using all available resources to perform an emergency landing. Although the aircraft crashed, the coordinated efforts of the crew saved many lives and demonstrated the value of CRM in managing extreme situations.

CRM has also been instrumental in everyday flight operations, where it helps prevent minor issues from escalating into major problems. By fostering a culture of open communication and collaboration, CRM ensures that potential safety threats are identified and addressed early, reducing the risk of accidents.

CRM Training and Its Importance

CRM training is mandatory for airline pilots and is an integral part of their professional development. The training typically includes both classroom instruction and practical exercises, such as simulated flight scenarios where crew members can practice their communication, decision-making, and teamwork skills in a controlled environment.

CRM training is not a one-time event; it is an ongoing process that is revisited throughout a pilot's career. Regular refresher courses ensure that pilots stay up-to-date with the latest CRM practices and are continually improving their skills. These courses often incorporate lessons learned from recent incidents and accidents, making the training relevant and timely.

Moreover, CRM principles are increasingly being integrated into other aspects of aviation, such as maintenance and ground operations. This holistic approach recognizes that safety is a shared responsibility and that effective communication and teamwork are essential at all levels of the operation.

Conclusion

Crew Resource Management has revolutionized the way aviation professionals approach safety and teamwork. By emphasizing communication, teamwork, decision-making, situational awareness, and workload management, CRM has made flying safer and more efficient. Its principles have become a fundamental part of aviation culture, ensuring that pilots and crew are better equipped to handle the complexities of modern flight operations.

As aviation continues to evolve, CRM will remain a critical component of pilot training and operations, helping to prevent accidents and save lives. The success of CRM in aviation also serves as a model for other high-stakes industries, demonstrating the power of collaboration and effective resource management in achieving safety and excellence.

Emergency Procedures and Management

Emergency procedures are a critical aspect of aviation safety. Pilots must be prepared to handle a variety of unexpected situations, from engine failures to medical emergencies on board. This chapter will provide a detailed overview of emergency procedures and management, emphasizing the importance of preparation, quick decision-making, and effective communication.

Understanding Emergency Procedures

Effective emergency management is based on three key principles:

Aviate, Navigate, Communicate.

- **Aviate:** The first priority in any emergency is to maintain control of the aircraft. This means ensuring that the aircraft is flying safely and stably before addressing any other issues.

- **Navigate:** Once the aircraft is under control, the next step is to determine the best course of action. This may involve finding a suitable landing site, navigating to an alternate airport, or following specific emergency routes.

- **Communicate:** Effective communication with air traffic control (**ATC**) and the cabin crew is essential. Informing ATC of the situation allows them to provide assistance and clear the airspace if necessary.

Common Emergency Scenarios and Procedures

Here are some common emergency scenarios and the procedures typically followed:

1. **Engine Failure:**
   - Immediate Actions: Maintain control of the aircraft, reduce drag by adjusting the pitch and configuration, and attempt to restart the engine if possible.
   - Navigation: Identify the nearest suitable landing site, such as an airport or open field.
   - Communication: Declare an emergency with ATC, providing your position, altitude, and intentions.

2. **Electrical System Failure:**

    - Immediate Actions: Switch to backup electrical systems if available, and prioritize essential instruments and systems.

    - Navigation: Use manual navigation methods if electronic systems are compromised.

    - Communication: Inform ATC of the failure and request assistance as needed.

3. **Fire on Board:**

    - Immediate Actions: Identify the source of the fire and use appropriate fire suppression methods. If the fire is in the cabin, follow procedures for smoke evacuation and passenger management.

    - Navigation: Land as soon as possible at the nearest suitable airport.

    - Communication: Declare an emergency and provide details of the fire to ATC.

4. **Medical Emergency:**

    - Immediate Actions: Assess the situation and provide first aid if possible. Use onboard medical kits and follow any available medical guidance.

    - Navigation: Decide whether to continue to the destination or divert to the nearest airport with medical facilities.

    - Communication: Inform ATC of the medical emergency and request priority handling if necessary.

Decision-Making in Emergencies

Quick and effective decision-making is crucial in emergencies. Pilots are trained to use the *DECIDE Model:*

1. **Detect:** Recognize that an emergency exists.

2. **Estimate:** Evaluate the situation and determine the best course of action.

3. **Choose:** Select the most appropriate action based on the evaluation.

4. **Identify:** Identify the steps needed to implement the chosen action.

5. **Do:** Execute the chosen action.

6. **Evaluate:** Assess the effectiveness of the action and make adjustments if necessary.

Training and Preparation

Regular training and preparation are essential for effective emergency management. This includes:

- **Simulator Training:** Practicing emergency procedures in a flight simulator helps pilots develop the skills and confidence needed to handle real-life situations.

- **Checklists:** Using emergency checklists ensures that all necessary steps are followed in the correct order.

- **Briefings:** Pre-flight briefings should include a review of emergency procedures and the location of emergency equipment.

Emergency procedures and management are vital components of aviation safety. By understanding the key principles, practicing common procedures, and engaging in regular training, pilots can effectively handle emergencies and ensure the safety of their aircraft and passengers. Quick decision-making, effective communication, and thorough preparation are the cornerstones of successful emergency management.

ETOPS

ETOPS (**Extended-range Twin-engine Operational Performance Standards**) is a crucial concept in modern aviation, particularly for long-haul flights operated by twin-engine aircraft. ETOPS regulations allow twin-engine planes to fly routes that are farther from the nearest suitable airport than previously permitted. This chapter explores the origins, regulations, and operational significance of ETOPS.

What is ETOPS?

ETOPS is a set of rules and regulations developed by the International Civil Aviation Organization (**ICAO**) and adopted by aviation authorities worldwide, including the Federal Aviation Administration (**FAA**) and the European Union Aviation Safety Agency (**EASA**). These standards allow twin-engine aircraft to operate on routes that take them more than 60 minutes away from an alternate airport, which is the standard limitation for twin-engine aircraft without ETOPS certification.

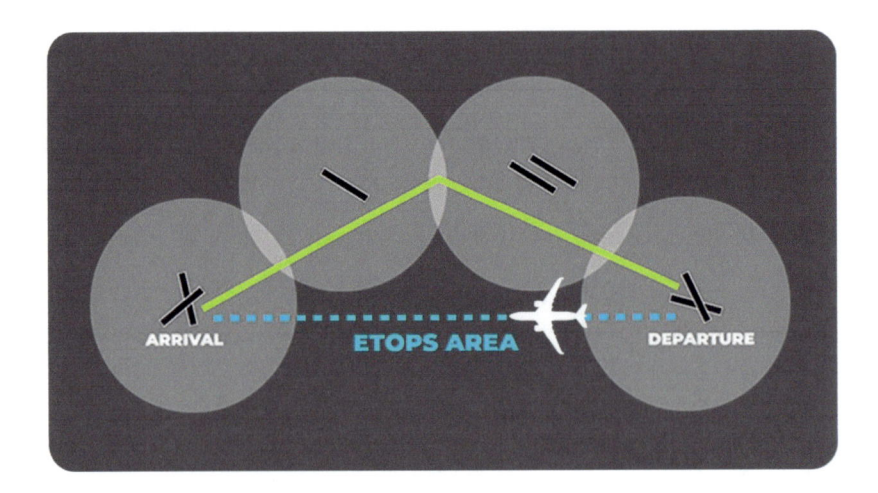

History and Development

The ETOPS concept emerged from the need to make long-distance travel more efficient and economical. Traditionally, long-haul routes were dominated by four-engine aircraft, which were not restricted by the same regulations as twin-engine planes. However, advancements in engine reliability and technology led to the recognition that twin-engine aircraft could safely operate over longer distances.

- 1985: The FAA introduced the first ETOPS regulations, allowing twin-engine aircraft to fly routes up to 120 minutes from a diversion airport.
- 1990s: ETOPS regulations were extended to 180 minutes, enabling more extensive route networks.
- Present Day: Modern ETOPS certifications can extend beyond 180 minutes, with some aircraft approved for up to 370 minutes, covering virtually any point on Earth.

ETOPS Certification

Requirements:

To obtain ETOPS certification, both the aircraft and the airline must meet stringent requirements:

- **Aircraft Certification:** The aircraft must demonstrate exceptional reliability and performance standards, particularly regarding its engines and critical systems.
- **Maintenance Programs:** Enhanced maintenance procedures must be implemented, including more frequent and detailed inspections.
- **Flight Crew Training:** Pilots and crew must undergo specialized training to handle potential ETOPS scenarios, including engine failures and diversions.

Levels of ETOPS Certification:

ETOPS certifications are typically categorized by the number of minutes the aircraft is allowed to be from an alternate airport. Common ETOPS certifications include:

- **ETOPS-120:** 120 minutes from a suitable airport
- **ETOPS-240 and beyond:** Extending up to 370 minutes, depending on the aircraft and operational needs

Operational Significance

ETOPS has transformed the operational landscape of the aviation industry, offering several significant benefits:

Route Flexibility

ETOPS allows airlines to operate more direct routes across vast oceans and remote regions, reducing flight times and fuel consumption. This flexibility enables airlines to offer non-stop services between distant city pairs, enhancing convenience for passengers.

Economic Efficiency

Twin-engine aircraft are generally more fuel-efficient and cost-effective to operate compared to their four-engine counterparts. ETOPS certification enables airlines to maximize these efficiencies on long-haul routes, resulting in lower operating costs and increased profitability.

Environmental Impact

By enabling more direct flight paths and using fuel-efficient twin-engine aircraft, ETOPS contributes to reduced greenhouse gas emissions and a lower environmental footprint for the aviation industry.

ETOPS represents a pivotal advancement in aviation, enabling twin-engine aircraft to safely and efficiently operate on long-haul routes that were once the domain of four-engine planes. By understanding the requirements, benefits, and operational considerations of ETOPS, airlines can enhance their route networks, reduce costs, and provide better services to passengers. As technology continues to evolve, ETOPS will likely play an even more significant role in shaping the future of global air travel.

Decision Altitude (DA) and Decision Height (DH)

In instrument flying, precision and timely decision-making are essential, especially during an approach to landing in low-visibility conditions. Two key concepts that pilots must understand in this context are Decision Altitude (**DA**) and Decision Height (**DH**). These terms are often used interchangeably but have distinct meanings and applications, depending on the type of approach and the system used.

What are Decision Altitude (DA) and Decision Height (DH)?

Decision Altitude (**DA**) is the specified altitude above mean sea level (**MSL**) during a precision approach, at which a pilot must decide whether to continue the descent and land or to execute a missed approach. If the required visual references for landing (**such as the runway or approach lights**) are not in sight when the aircraft reaches the DA, the pilot must initiate a missed approach immediately.

Decision Height (**DH**), on the other hand, is the specified height above the ground (above the runway threshold or touchdown zone) at which this decision must be made. DH is typically used in conjunction with radio altimeter readings, which measure the aircraft's height above terrain, rather than its altitude above sea level.

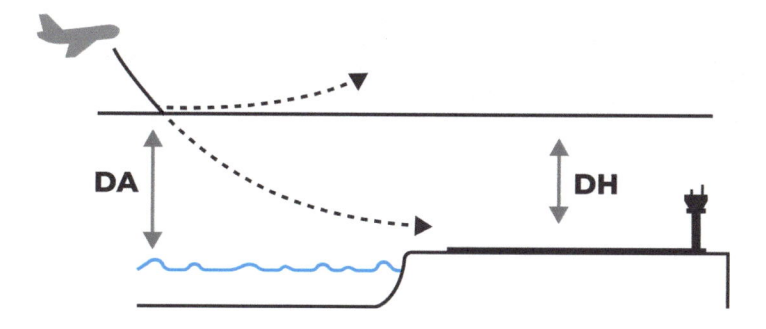

How DA and DH are Determined

DA and DH are both established based on safety requirements, ensuring sufficient clearance from obstacles and allowing the pilot adequate time to respond if a missed approach is necessary. The determination of DA or DH takes into account the type of approach, the airport's terrain, and the precision of the approach systems.

Safety and Operational Procedures | 191

- **Type of Approach:** For most precision approaches, like an Instrument Landing System (**ILS**) approach, DA is commonly used. The specific DA is published on the approach chart and varies depending on the category of the approach (**e.g., CAT I, CAT II, CAT III**). For example, a CAT I ILS approach typically has a DA around 200 feet above the touchdown zone elevation (**TDZE**).

- **Radio Altimeter Use:** DH is typically used in lower category approaches (such as CAT II and CAT III ILS approaches), where more precise height information is critical due to the very low visibility conditions. The radio altimeter provides real-time height data, allowing pilots to adhere to the DH during such approaches.

- **Obstacle Clearance and Terrain:** Both DA and DH ensure that the aircraft remains safely above any obstacles in the approach path. The altitude or height is calculated to provide sufficient clearance, even if the pilot must execute a missed approach.

Decision-Making at DA or DH

Reaching DA or DH is a pivotal moment in an instrument approach. The pilot must quickly assess whether the necessary visual references are visible and if the aircraft is properly aligned with the runway for a safe landing. This decision must be made promptly to ensure safety.

- **Visual References:** At DA or DH, the pilot needs to confirm the presence of essential visual cues, such as the runway, approach lights, or threshold markings. If these references are clearly visible and the aircraft is in a stable landing configuration, the pilot may continue the approach to landing.

- **Missed Approach Procedure:** If the visual references are not in sight by the time the aircraft reaches DA or DH, the pilot must execute a missed approach. This procedure is critical for avoiding obstacles and ensuring that the aircraft can safely attempt another approach or divert to an alternate airport.

The Difference Between DA and DH

While DA and DH serve similar purposes, their key difference lies in how they are measured:

- **DA (Decision Altitude):** Measured in altitude above mean sea level (**MSL**), DA is used when barometric altimeters are the primary source of altitude information. It is most commonly associated with CAT I precision approaches.

- **DH (Decision Height):** Measured as height above the runway threshold or touchdown zone, DH is typically used in conjunction with radio altimeters, particularly in CAT II and CAT III approaches. These approaches require more precise altitude information due to the lower visibility conditions involved.

Importance of Strict Adherence to DA and DH

Strict adherence to DA or DH is essential for maintaining safety during instrument approaches. Continuing below these altitudes or heights without the required visual references can lead to dangerous situations, including controlled flight into terrain (**CFIT**) or hard landings.

- **Training and Practice:** Pilots receive extensive training to correctly interpret and respond to DA or DH. Simulated approaches and regular practice ensure that pilots are proficient in making the correct decisions at these critical points.

- **Technological Aids:** Modern avionics often include alerts or annunciations as the aircraft approaches DA or DH, helping pilots prepare for the decision point. However, it is the pilot's responsibility to remain vigilant and prepared to execute the missed approach if necessary.

Decision Altitude (**DA**) and Decision Height (**DH**) are integral components of safe instrument flying. These thresholds ensure that pilots have a clear point at which they must decide whether to continue the approach or execute a missed approach based on the visibility of the runway environment. Understanding the difference between DA and DH, and the circumstances under which each is used, is crucial for every pilot operating in instrument meteorological conditions. By adhering to these standards, pilots can significantly enhance the safety and reliability of their flight operations.

Chapter 9

Human Factors and Decision-Making

Human Factors in Aviation

Human factors play a critical role in aviation safety and efficiency. Understanding how human capabilities and limitations impact performance is essential for minimizing errors and enhancing safety. This chapter explores the various aspects of human factors in aviation, including cognitive, physical, and organizational elements, and how they influence flight operations.

The Importance of Human Factors

Human factors refer to the study of how humans interact with systems, equipment, and procedures. In aviation, this involves understanding how pilots, air traffic controllers, maintenance personnel, and other stakeholders perform their tasks and how their performance can be optimized.

Cognitive Factors

Cognitive factors involve mental processes such as perception, memory, decision-making, and attention. Key aspects include:

Situational Awareness: Maintaining an accurate perception of the aircraft's state, environment, and future conditions. Loss of situational awareness can lead to errors and accidents.

Decision-Making: Pilots must make quick, accurate decisions, often under pressure. Training and experience are crucial for effective decision-making.

Workload Management: Balancing multiple tasks without becoming overwhelmed. High workload can lead to errors, while low workload can result in complacency.

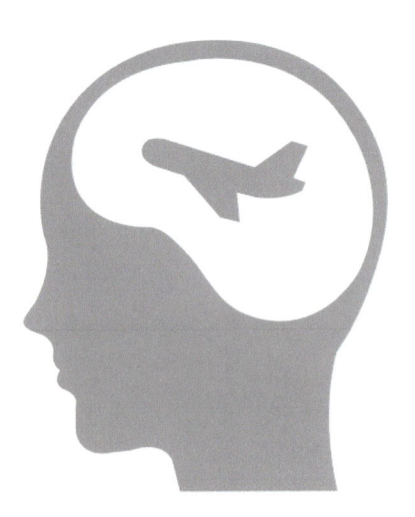

Physical Factors

Physical factors pertain to the human body's capabilities and limitations. Important considerations include:

1. **Fatigue:** Long duty hours, irregular schedules, and time zone changes can lead to fatigue, impairing cognitive and physical performance.

2. **Health and Fitness:** Maintaining good physical health is essential for handling the demands of flying, especially during emergencies.

3. **Ergonomics:** Designing cockpits and controls to fit human physical characteristics can reduce strain and improve performance.

Organizational Factors

Organizational factors involve the structures, policies, and cultures within aviation organizations. Key elements include:

1. **Crew Resource Management (CRM):** Training programs that enhance communication, teamwork, and decision-making among flight crews.

2. **Safety Culture:** An organizational commitment to safety, encouraging reporting of errors and near-misses without fear of retribution.

3. **Regulatory Compliance:** Adhering to regulations and standards set by aviation authorities to ensure safety and efficiency.

Human Error

Human error is a significant factor in aviation incidents and accidents. Understanding the types of errors can help in developing strategies to mitigate them:

1. **Slips and Lapses:** Unintentional errors, such as forgetting to complete a checklist item.

2. **Mistakes:** Errors in judgment or decision-making, often due to incorrect information or assumptions.

3. **Violations:** Deliberate deviations from procedures, which can be routine or exceptional.

Mitigating Human Factors Issues

Several strategies can be employed to mitigate human factors issues:

1. **Training and Simulation:** Regular training and realistic simulations can prepare crews for various scenarios and improve their skills.

2. **Standard Operating Procedures (SOPs):** Clear, well-defined procedures help reduce variability and ensure consistency.

3. **Automation and Technology:** Advanced systems can assist pilots and reduce workload, but it's essential to maintain manual flying skills.

4. **Fatigue Management:** Implementing policies to manage duty hours and rest periods can help mitigate fatigue-related errors.

Human factors are integral to aviation safety and performance. By understanding and addressing cognitive, physical, and organizational elements, the aviation industry can reduce errors and enhance safety. Continuous training, effective communication, and a strong safety culture are essential components in managing human factors.

This chapter has provided an overview of the critical aspects of human factors in aviation. Mastery of these concepts is vital for anyone involved in aviation operations, from pilots and air traffic controllers to maintenance personnel and organizational leaders.

Aircraft Fuel Systems

The fuel system is one of the most critical components of an aircraft, ensuring that the engines receive a consistent and reliable supply of fuel. This chapter delves into the intricacies of aircraft fuel systems, covering their design, operation, and the various types of fuel used in aviation. Understanding these systems is essential for ensuring flight safety and efficiency.

Components of Aircraft Fuel Systems

Aircraft fuel systems are complex and consist of several key components:

1. **Fuel Tanks:** These are storage units located in the wings, fuselage, or tail of the aircraft. They are designed to hold large quantities of fuel while maintaining the aircraft's balance.

2. **Fuel Pumps:** These ensure a steady flow of fuel from the tanks to the engines. There are typically both electric and engine-driven pumps for redundancy.

3. **Fuel Lines:** These are the conduits through which fuel travels from the tanks to the engines. They must be durable and resistant to leaks.

4. **Fuel Filters:** These remove impurities from the fuel, preventing damage to the engines.

5. **Fuel Gauges and Sensors:** These provide real-time information on fuel quantity, pressure, and temperature, crucial for flight management.

6. **Fuel Control Units:** These regulate the amount of fuel entering the engine, ensuring optimal performance.

Types of Aviation Fuel

Different types of aircraft require different types of fuel:

1. **Jet Fuel (Jet A, Jet A-1):** Used by turbine engine aircraft, including commercial jets. Jet A-1 has a lower freezing point than Jet A, making it suitable for long-haul flights.

2. **Jet B:** A wide-cut fuel that is a blend of gasoline and kerosene. It has a lower flash point and is more volatile than Jet A/A-1, making it suitable for use in extremely cold climates. It is less commonly used but is still operational in some regions, particularly in military and remote areas.

3. **Avgas (Aviation Gasoline):** Used by piston-engine aircraft, typically smaller planes and helicopters. Avgas has a higher octane rating than automotive gasoline.

4. **Biofuels:** Emerging as a sustainable alternative, biofuels are derived from renewable sources and can be blended with conventional jet fuel.

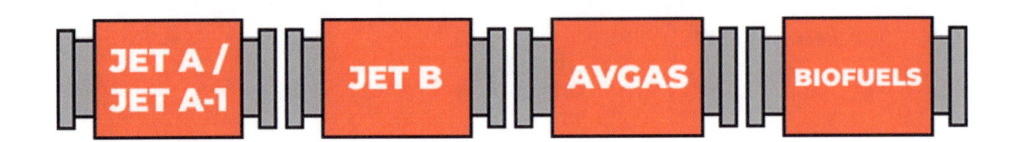

Fuel Management

Effective fuel management is crucial for flight safety and efficiency:

- **Fuel Planning:** Calculating the required amount of fuel for a flight, including reserves for contingencies.

- **Fuel Transfer:** Moving fuel between tanks to maintain the aircraft's balance and stability.

- **Fuel Monitoring:** Continuously monitoring fuel levels and consumption rates to ensure the aircraft has enough fuel to reach its destination.

Safety Features

Aircraft fuel systems are equipped with several safety features:

- **Fuel Shutoff Valves:** These can isolate sections of the fuel system in case of a leak or fire.

- **Fire Suppression Systems:** These are designed to extinguish fires in the fuel tanks or engine compartments.

- **Redundant Systems:** Multiple pumps and fuel lines ensure that the engine continues to receive fuel even if one component fails.

Maintenance and Inspection

Regular maintenance and inspection are vital for the reliability of fuel systems:

1. **Routine Checks:** Inspecting fuel lines, filters, and tanks for leaks or damage.
2. **Fuel Quality Testing:** Ensuring the fuel is free from contaminants and meets the required specifications.
3. **System Calibration:** Verifying that fuel gauges and sensors provide accurate readings.

Aircraft fuel systems are integral to the safe and efficient operation of any aircraft. By understanding the components, types of fuel, and management practices, aviation professionals can ensure that these systems perform reliably under all conditions. Regular maintenance, safety features, and environmental considerations further enhance the reliability and sustainability of fuel systems.

Environmental Control System (ECS)

The Environmental Control System (**ECS**) is a critical system in any aircraft that ensures the comfort of passengers and the safety of the crew. It maintains a comfortable cabin environment by regulating temperature, air pressure, and air quality under various flight conditions. In this chapter, we will explore the main functions and components of the ECS and its significance for flight operations.

Main Functions of the ECS

The ECS serves several important functions, including:

- **Temperature Control:** The ECS regulates the cabin temperature to create a comfortable climate, which is essential as outside temperatures can be extremely low at high altitudes.
- **Pressure Regulation:** At high altitudes, the air pressure is significantly lower than at sea level. The ECS ensures that cabin pressure is maintained at a level that is comfortable and safe for passengers and crew.
- **Air Circulation and Quality:** The system continuously circulates fresh air in the cabin and filters pollutants to maintain good air quality.

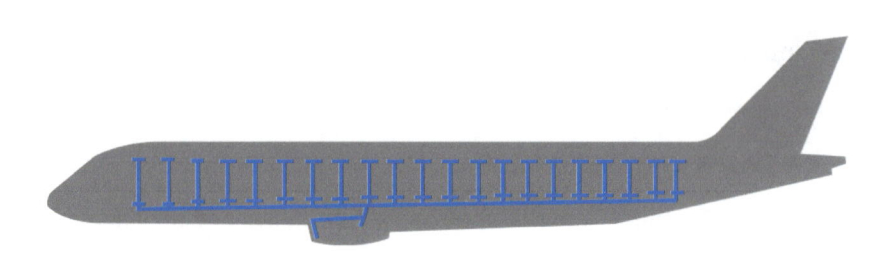

Key Components of the ECS

The ECS consists of several key components that work together to perform the above functions:

- **Air Compressors:** These compress outside air to generate the necessary pressure for the cabin.
- **Conditioning Units:** These units regulate the temperature of the air by either cooling or heating it, depending on the cabin's requirements.
- **Air Filters:** The filters remove dirt, dust, and other particles from the air before it enters the cabin.
- **Distribution Ducts:** These ducts evenly distribute the treated air throughout the cabin to ensure consistent airflow.
- **Control Systems:** Modern aircraft are equipped with advanced control systems that automatically adjust ECS settings based on current conditions.

How the ECS Works

The ECS typically begins with the compression of outside air by the engines or dedicated compressors. The compressed air is then routed through the conditioning units, where it is cooled or heated as necessary. The filtered and conditioned air is subsequently distributed into the cabin via the ducts.

Cabin pressure and temperature sensors continuously monitor the conditions within the cabin. Control systems can make adjustments as needed to ensure that the cabin remains in a comfortable state.

Importance of the ECS for Flight Safety

The ECS is not only essential for passenger comfort but also for safety. A properly functioning ECS ensures that the cabin remains pressurized, preventing hypoxia (**oxygen deficiency**). In the event of a pressure loss or ECS failure, crew members must immediately implement emergency procedures to safeguard everyone on board.

Challenges and Maintenance of the ECS

The ECS faces several challenges, including extreme temperatures and high altitudes. Regular maintenance and inspections are critical to ensure that all components function correctly. When anomalies occur in the ECS, technicians often need to perform diagnostics to quickly address issues.

The Environmental Control System (**ECS**) plays a vital role in modern aircraft design. It not only provides comfort for passengers but also ensures their safety during flight. Understanding the operation and components of the ECS is crucial for anyone interested in aviation.

Pressurization and Oxygen Systems

Flying at high altitudes presents unique challenges for both the aircraft and its occupants. As aircraft ascend, air pressure decreases, making it harder to breathe due to lower oxygen levels. To maintain a safe and comfortable environment, modern aircraft use pressurization systems to keep cabin pressure at a level where passengers and crew can breathe normally. Additionally, oxygen systems provide supplemental oxygen in emergency situations. This chapter explores how these systems work and their importance for safe flight.

Why Pressurization is Necessary

At sea level, the atmosphere exerts approximately 1013.25 hPa (**hectopascals**) of pressure. As an aircraft climbs, atmospheric pressure decreases rapidly. For example, at an altitude of 35,000 feet, air pressure is about one-quarter of that at sea level, and the oxygen levels in the air are too low to sustain human life without assistance.

Effects of Low Pressure on the Human Body:

- **Hypoxia:** A lack of sufficient oxygen in the bloodstream, which can cause dizziness, confusion, or unconsciousness.

- **Barotrauma:** Damage to body tissues due to changes in pressure, affecting areas such as the ears, sinuses, and lungs.

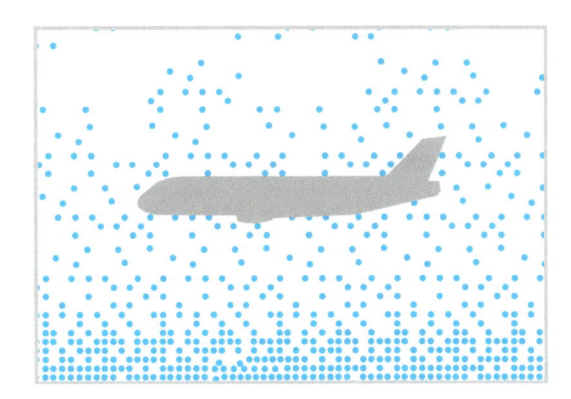

Pressurization ensures that the cabin remains at a safe atmospheric pressure, typically equivalent to altitudes of 6,000 to 8,000 feet, even when the aircraft flies at much higher altitudes.

How Aircraft Pressurization Systems Work

Aircraft pressurization systems control the cabin pressure by pumping conditioned air into the cabin. This air is usually drawn from the engine's compressor section (known as bleed air) or from a dedicated air-conditioning pack.

Components of a Pressurization System:

- **Outflow Valve:** The main control component for maintaining cabin pressure. It regulates the amount of air leaving the cabin to control the internal pressure.

- **Pressure Controllers:** These are automatic systems that monitor cabin altitude and adjust the outflow valve to maintain the desired pressure.

- **Cabin Pressure Indicators:** Instruments in the cockpit display the current cabin pressure, altitude, and the rate of change. Pilots monitor these indicators during flight.

Pressurization Phases:

1. **Ground Phase:** While on the ground, the aircraft cabin is not pressurized. The system remains inactive until takeoff.

2. **Climb Phase:** As the aircraft climbs, the cabin pressurization system gradually increases the cabin pressure to simulate an altitude of 6,000–8,000 feet, even as the aircraft reaches cruising altitude.

3. **Cruise Phase:** The system maintains a constant cabin pressure, while the aircraft flies at altitudes between 30,000 and 40,000 feet.

4. **Descent Phase:** During descent, the system gradually reduces cabin pressure to match the external air pressure at lower altitudes.

Cabin Pressure Control Modes

Modern aircraft use both automatic and manual pressurization modes. In automatic mode, the system adjusts the pressure without pilot intervention. Manual mode is used if the automatic system fails, allowing the pilot to control the outflow valve manually.

- **Automatic Mode:** Typically, two controllers operate independently for redundancy. The system adjusts based on the aircraft's altitude and rate of ascent or descent.

- **Manual Mode:** Pilots control the outflow valve via cockpit switches, using visual cues from cabin pressure instruments.

Cabin Pressurization Safety Features

Aircraft are equipped with multiple safety features to prevent or address pressurization issues:

- **Safety Valves:** These valves prevent the cabin from becoming over-pressurized by releasing excess air if the pressure exceeds a certain limit.

- **Pressure Relief Valves:** Prevents under-pressurization, allowing air to enter the cabin if external pressure becomes too low.

- **Emergency Pressure Dump Switch:** Allows pilots to rapidly depressurize the cabin in an emergency, typically used in fire or smoke situations.

Oxygen Systems in Aircraft

While pressurization systems maintain a breathable environment during normal operations, aircraft are also equipped with emergency oxygen systems in case of pressurization failure. These systems provide supplemental oxygen to both passengers and crew.

Oxygen for Passengers

In the event of cabin depressurization, the oxygen masks will deploy automatically from overhead compartments.

How It Works:

- **Chemical Oxygen Generators:** In many commercial aircraft, a chemical reaction generates oxygen. When a mask is pulled down, it activates the generator, providing about 12-20 minutes of oxygen, which is usually enough time for the aircraft to descend to a safe altitude.

- **Flow Indicators:** Passengers can see the oxygen flowing by checking the bag attached to the mask. Even if the bag doesn't inflate, oxygen is still being supplied.

Oxygen for Crew

Pilots and cabin crew have access to more robust oxygen systems:

- **Pressurized Oxygen Tanks:** Unlike the chemical generators used for passengers, pilots have access to pressurized oxygen tanks that provide a constant flow of oxygen for the duration of an emergency.

- **Quick-Donning Masks:** Flight crew masks are designed for rapid deployment and allow pilots to don them within seconds. These masks provide both oxygen and protection from smoke.

Types of Oxygen Systems

There are three main types of oxygen systems used in aviation:

- **Continuous Flow:** Used in passenger masks, it provides a constant flow of oxygen at all altitudes.

- **Diluter Demand:** Common in cockpit masks, this system mixes oxygen with cabin air, adjusting the oxygen ratio based on altitude to conserve oxygen.

- **Pressure Demand:** Used at very high altitudes, this system forces oxygen into the lungs at higher-than-normal pressure, ensuring adequate oxygenation even in thin air.

Cabin Depressurization Emergencies

In the rare event of a depressurization emergency, the following procedures are critical:

- **Rapid Descent:** The aircraft will descend rapidly to an altitude of 10,000 feet or lower, where supplemental oxygen is no longer required.

- **Oxygen Mask Deployment:** Masks will deploy automatically, and passengers must secure their masks before assisting others.

- **Communication with ATC:** Pilots will notify Air Traffic Control of the emergency and request priority clearance to descend.

Pressurization and oxygen systems are critical for maintaining a safe and comfortable environment in flight, particularly at high altitudes where low atmospheric pressure can be life-threatening. These systems are designed with multiple safety features and redundancies to ensure that passengers and crew can breathe normally, even in emergency situations. Understanding how these systems work is essential for both pilots and aviation enthusiasts alike, as they play a pivotal role in modern flight operations.

Deicing and Anti-Icing Systems

Aircraft operations in cold weather conditions bring unique challenges, including the accumulation of ice on critical surfaces such as wings, tail, and engine inlets. Ice can significantly impact an aircraft's performance, reduce lift, increase drag, and potentially cause dangerous situations. To combat these effects, modern aircraft are equipped with deicing and anti-icing systems designed to prevent or remove ice build-up during flight and on the ground. This chapter covers how these systems work, their components, and why they are crucial for safe flight operations.

The Dangers of Ice Accumulation

Ice formation on an aircraft can occur in several ways, but the most common form is supercooled liquid water droplets in clouds or fog. When these droplets strike an aircraft flying through them, they freeze upon contact. This can lead to:

- **Reduced Lift:** Ice changes the shape of the wing and tail, disrupting airflow and reducing lift generation.

- **Increased Drag:** Ice increases surface roughness, creating more drag, which can reduce the aircraft's performance and fuel efficiency.

- **Control Problems:** Ice can alter the aerodynamics of control surfaces like ailerons, elevators, and rudders, making it harder for the pilot to maneuver the aircraft.

- **Engine Damage:** Ice ingestion into engines can lead to compressor stalls or damage to internal components.

Because of these risks, deicing and anti-icing systems are essential for preventing dangerous ice build-up during various phases of flight.

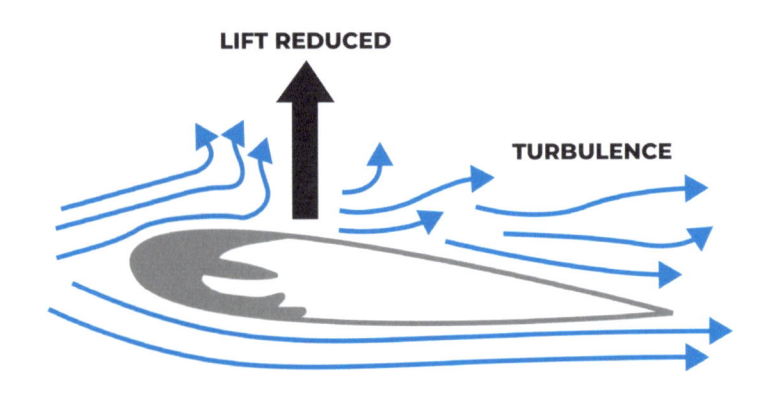

Deicing vs. Anti-Icing: What's the Difference?

Although often used interchangeably, deicing and anti-icing refer to two different approaches to handling ice accumulation:

- **Deicing:** Refers to the removal of existing ice after it has formed on an aircraft. This is usually done on the ground before takeoff using deicing fluids or specialized equipment.

- **Anti-Icing:** Prevents ice from forming in the first place. This can be accomplished both in the air and on the ground by applying heat or chemicals that inhibit ice formation.

Deicing Systems

Ground-Based Deicing

Before an aircraft takes off in icy or snowy conditions, deicing must be performed on the ground. This process typically involves spraying the aircraft with deicing fluids to remove ice, snow, or frost from critical surfaces.

- **Deicing Fluids:** The most commonly used deicing fluid is Type I fluid, which is a glycol-based solution mixed with water. This fluid is heated and sprayed on the aircraft to melt and remove ice.

- **Other Types of Fluids:**
    - Type II and IV Fluids: These are thickened, slower-draining anti-icing fluids used after deicing to prevent further accumulation of ice during takeoff. They remain on the aircraft longer to protect critical surfaces until the aircraft reaches higher altitudes where icing is less of a concern.

Deicing Procedure

- The aircraft is positioned in a designated deicing area.
- Ground crews spray the aircraft with heated Type I fluid, removing any existing ice.
- If necessary, Type IV fluid is applied to prevent further icing during takeoff.

Pneumatic Boot Deicing Systems

Many aircraft, particularly turboprop planes, use pneumatic deicing boots installed on the leading edges of wings and tail surfaces. These boots consist of rubber strips that can be inflated and deflated in cycles.

How it Works

- During flight, when ice forms on the leading edges, the boots are inflated using air from the aircraft's pneumatic system.
- The inflation of the boots causes ice to crack and break off from the surface.
- Afterward, the boots deflate and return to their normal shape.

This system is effective but can only be used intermittently, as it doesn't prevent ice from forming, but rather removes it after accumulation.

Anti-Icing Systems

Thermal Anti-Icing Systems

Thermal anti-icing systems use heat to prevent ice formation on critical areas like engine inlets and wing leading edges. These systems are most commonly found on jet aircraft, which use bleed air from the engines to generate heat.

How it Works:

- Hot air is bled from the engine's compressor section and directed through ducts to the leading edges of the wings, tail, or engine nacelles.
- The heat keeps these surfaces warm enough to prevent ice from forming.
- On some aircraft, electric heaters are used in smaller areas like pitot tubes, windshields, and propeller blades.

This method is highly effective for preventing ice from forming, but it requires a lot of energy, which can slightly reduce engine performance.

Electric Anti-Icing Systems

In certain areas of the aircraft, like the cockpit windshield and pitot-static tubes, electric heating elements are used to prevent ice accumulation.

Windshield Heating:

- Transparent conductive coatings or embedded heating elements are integrated into the aircraft's windshield.
- These systems prevent ice from forming and maintain visibility for the pilots.

Pitot-Static Heating

- Pitot tubes, which measure airspeed, and static ports, which provide altitude information, are equipped with small electrical heaters to ensure they remain ice-free.

Electric anti-icing systems are lightweight and effective, especially for smaller components where bleed air systems would be impractical.

Engine Anti-Icing

Engines are particularly vulnerable to ice build-up, especially at the inlets, which could lead to engine flameouts or damage. To prevent this, most aircraft use engine anti-icing systems that heat the engine's air intake areas.

- **Jet Engines:** Bleed air from the engine's compressor is routed to the inlet cowling, keeping it warm to prevent ice formation.
- **Propeller Aircraft:** Propeller blades may be equipped with electric de-icers or fluid-based anti-icing systems, which prevent ice from forming on the propeller surfaces.

Ice Detection Systems

Some aircraft are equipped with ice detection systems that automatically activate deicing or anti-icing measures when ice is detected. These systems use probes on the exterior of the aircraft to sense the accumulation of ice. When a certain amount of ice is detected, the system alerts the pilot or automatically turns on the anti-icing systems.

Icing in Flight and the Role of Pilots

Despite the presence of anti-icing and deicing systems, pilots must remain vigilant in icing conditions. Pilots receive training to recognize the signs of icing and understand how to safely navigate these environments.

In-Flight Considerations:

- Pilots must activate anti-icing systems as soon as icing conditions are encountered.
- If severe icing is experienced, the safest course of action is usually to change altitude or exit the icing conditions by altering the flight path.

Regulations and Safety

Both international and national aviation authorities, such as the FAA and EASA, have strict regulations regarding icing conditions and the use of deicing and anti-icing systems. Aircraft must undergo rigorous testing to ensure their systems are capable of handling various icing scenarios.

Additionally, pilots must adhere to Aircraft Flight Manual (**AFM**) procedures for using deicing and anti-icing systems, including when to activate these systems and how to manage icing risks during all phases of flight.

Chapter 10

Environmental Impact and Innovations

Aviation and Climate Change

The aviation industry is at a crossroads. While air travel connects the world like never before, it also contributes significantly to climate change, accounting for 2–3% of global CO_2 emissions. To address this, the industry is exploring alternative propulsion systems, including Sustainable Aviation Fuel (**SAF**), hydrogen, and electric power. This chapter examines these technologies, their potential, and the challenges they face in revolutionizing aviation.

Sustainable Aviation Fuel (SAF)

SAF is the aviation industry's most viable short-term solution to reduce carbon emissions. Made from renewable feedstocks like used cooking oil, algae, or synthetic processes, SAF can be blended with conventional jet fuel and used in existing aircraft engines. Its "drop-in" nature avoids the need for costly infrastructure changes, making it a practical choice for airlines aiming to meet emissions targets.

Advantages:

- Reduces lifecycle CO_2 emissions by up to 80% compared to fossil fuels.
- Compatible with current aircraft and fueling infrastructure.
- Supported by policies like the EU's ReFuelEU Aviation mandate (**5% SAF by 2030**).

Challenges:

- High production costs (**2–5x more expensive than conventional fuel**).
- Limited feedstock availability and competition with food crops.

Hydrogen

Hydrogen offers a zero-emission future for aviation. It can be used in two ways: combusted in modified engines or converted to electricity via fuel cells. Airbus's ZEROe concept envisions hydrogen-powered aircraft by 2035, targeting regional and short-haul routes initially.

Pros:

- Zero CO_2 emissions (**only water vapor**).
- High energy density (**3x more energy per kg than jet fuel**).
- Suitable for long-haul flights with advanced storage solutions.

Cons:

- Requires cryogenic tanks (**-253°C**) or heavy pressurized systems.
- Airport infrastructure needs total overhaul (**e.g., hydrogen hubs**).

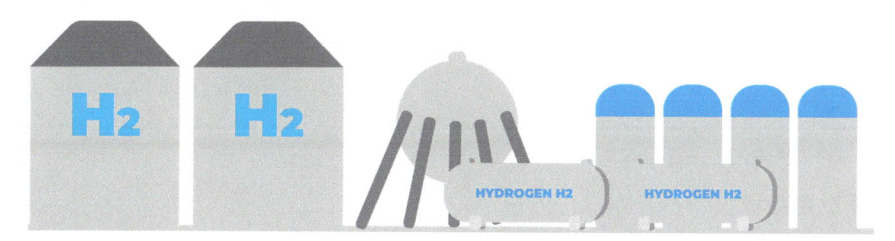

Electric Propulsion

Electric aircraft, powered by batteries, are ideal for short-haul flights and urban air mobility. Companies like Eviation (**Alice aircraft**) and Joby Aviation (**air taxis**) are pioneering this space, targeting emissions-free regional travel.

Advantages:

- Zero direct emissions and significantly quieter operations.
- Lower maintenance costs (**fewer moving parts than jet engines**).

Challenges:

- Battery limitations:
- Energy density 50x lower than jet fuel.
- Limited range (**e.g., 250 miles for a 9-seater**).
- Charging infrastructure requires airport grid upgrades.

Environmental Impact and Innovations | 215

Comparison Table: SAF vs. Hydrogen vs. Electric

ASPECT	SAF	HYDROGEN	ELECTRIC
Emissions	Up to 80% reduction	Zero CO_2 (water vapor only)	Zero direct emissions
Infrastructure	Compatible with existing systems	Requires new storage/refueling	Needs charging stations
Cost	2–5x more expensive	High (production/storage)	High (battery tech)
Best Use Case	Medium- to long-term bridging	Long-haul (post-2035)	Short-haul, urban air mobility
Example	United Airlines' SAF blends	Airbus ZEROe	Eviation Alice

The Path Forward

The aviation industry's decarbonization hinges on a three-pronged approach:

1. SAF for immediate emissions cuts.
2. Hydrogen for zero-emission long-haul travel.
3. Electric for regional and urban routes.

Critical Enablers:

- Government Support: Tax incentives, R&D funding, and mandates (**e.g., EU Green Deal**).
- Industry Collaboration: Airlines, manufacturers, and energy firms must align on standards.
- Public Acceptance: Educating travelers on the necessity of sustainable aviation.

The future of aviation lies in balancing innovation with practicality. While SAF bridges the gap today, hydrogen and electric technologies promise a cleaner tomorrow.

Introduction to Engine Chevrons

Have you ever noticed the serrated or zigzag pattern at the rear of some jet engines, like those on the Boeing 737 MAX? These features are called chevrons, and they are not just for aesthetics. Chevrons are a result of advanced engineering designed to reduce noise and improve the environmental performance of modern aircraft engines.

Introduction to Engine Chevrons

Chevrons are serrated edges located at the rear of a jet engine's nacelle or cowling, typically where the bypass air and hot exhaust gases exit the engine. These notches are part of the nacelle's design and are visible on many modern turbofan engines.

Why Do Engines Have Chevrons?

1. Noise Reduction

One of the primary reasons for chevrons is to reduce engine noise, particularly during takeoff and landing. Jet engines produce noise from two main sources:

- The interaction of high-speed exhaust gases with the surrounding air.
- The mixing of bypass air (**cooler air from the fan**) with the hot exhaust gases.

Chevrons smooth the mixing of these two airflows, reducing turbulence and noise. This effect is especially important for aircraft operating near urban areas where noise regulations are strict.

2. Compliance with Noise Regulations

Modern aviation faces stringent noise regulations set by organizations like the International Civil Aviation Organization (**ICAO**). Chevrons help manufacturers meet these standards by making engines quieter without compromising performance.

3. Improved Passenger Comfort

Reduced noise not only benefits communities near airports but also improves the flying experience for passengers. Quieter engines mean less cabin noise, making flights more comfortable.

How Do Chevrons Work?

Chevrons work by controlling how bypass air and exhaust gases mix as they exit the engine. Here's how the process works:

- **Airflow Interaction:** The serrated design creates small vortices (swirling air patterns) at the edges of the airflows.
- **Smoother Mixing:** These vortices smooth out the interaction between the bypass air and the hot exhaust gases.
- **Reduced Turbulence:** The smoother mixing reduces the intensity of turbulence, which is a major source of noise.

This design is a passive noise reduction method, meaning it doesn't rely on additional mechanical systems, making it lightweight and reliable.

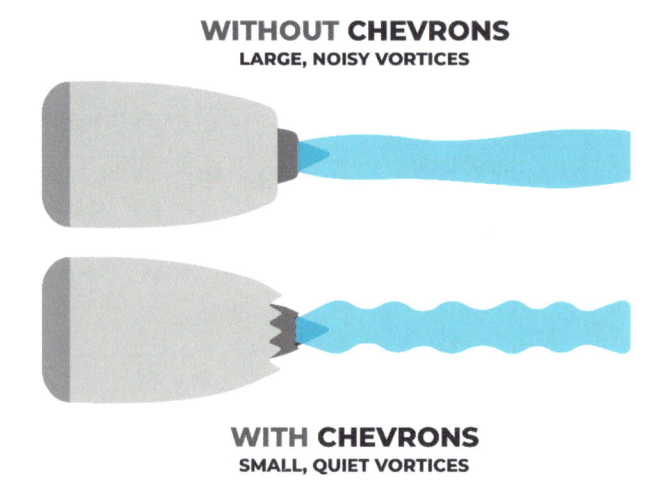

WITHOUT CHEVRONS
LARGE, NOISY VORTICES

WITH CHEVRONS
SMALL, QUIET VORTICES

Engine chevrons are a remarkable example of how modern engineering addresses environmental and regulatory challenges. By reducing noise pollution and enhancing passenger comfort, chevrons play a vital role in the advancement of quieter, more efficient air travel. The next time you see an aircraft with chevrons, you'll know the science behind those jagged edges and their impact on aviation.

Why Airplanes Are Mostly White?

When you look at commercial aircraft, one thing you'll notice is that most of them are painted white. This isn't just a matter of aesthetics; there are several practical reasons why white is the predominant color in aviation. Let's explore why airplanes are mostly white and the benefits that come with it.

Reflecting Sunlight and Reducing Heat

One of the primary reasons airplanes are painted white is to reflect sunlight. White surfaces reflect more sunlight and absorb less heat compared to darker colors. This is crucial for an airplane for several reasons:

- **Temperature Control:** Keeping the aircraft cooler helps reduce the load on the air conditioning systems, which is especially important when the plane is on the ground, as the internal temperature can rise quickly.
- **Material Protection:** By reflecting sunlight, white paint helps protect the aircraft's materials from the degrading effects of heat and UV radiation. This can extend the lifespan of the aircraft's structure and components.

Cost-Effectiveness

White paint is generally less expensive than other colors. Here's how it helps in cost management:

- **Paint Durability:** White paint tends to fade less over time compared to darker colors, which means the aircraft maintains its appearance longer and requires less frequent repainting. Repainting an aircraft is an expensive and time-consuming process, so extending the intervals between repaints can lead to significant cost savings.

- **Maintenance and Inspection:** White surfaces make it easier to spot damage, such as cracks, dents, and oil leaks. This simplifies maintenance inspections and enhances safety by ensuring that any issues are detected and addressed promptly.

Weight Considerations

Every additional layer of paint adds weight to the aircraft. While the difference in weight between white and darker paints might seem negligible, in aviation, every kilogram matters.

- **Fuel Efficiency:** A lighter aircraft consumes less fuel. Since fuel is one of the largest operating costs for airlines, even a small reduction in weight can lead to significant savings over the aircraft's lifetime.

Resale Value

Aircraft are often sold or leased several times over their lifespan. A white aircraft is more versatile in terms of branding and can easily be repainted or have decals added to suit the new owner's livery.

- **Neutral Color:** White is a neutral color that doesn't clash with airline branding and liveries. This makes it easier and cheaper for new owners to repaint the aircraft in their own colors.

Exceptions and Variations

While white is the most common color, there are exceptions. Some airlines choose to paint their planes in distinctive colors or special liveries for branding purposes, promotional events, or to commemorate special occasions.

- **Black and Dark Colors:** Although less common, some aircraft are painted in darker colors or black. These designs are often used for special liveries or VIP aircraft. However, they require more maintenance and can pose challenges in terms of heat management and visibility of damage.

In summary, the predominance of white in aircraft painting is due to its practical benefits, including better temperature control, cost-effectiveness, ease of maintenance, and increased resale value. While there are exceptions, the advantages of white paint make it the preferred choice for most airlines and aircraft manufacturers. So next time you see a white airplane, you'll know it's not just for looks—it's a smart choice driven by practicality and efficiency.

Chapter 11

Pilot Training and Career Pathways

Steps to Becoming a Pilot

Becoming a pilot is a dream for many, but it requires dedication, training, and a passion for aviation. While the exact process can vary from country to country, there are general steps that apply worldwide. This chapter outlines the typical path to becoming a commercial pilot, including essential qualifications, training, and licenses.

Step 1: You Need Money :´)

Let's get straight to the point: you need money. Becoming a pilot isn't cheap, and flight training can be a significant investment. But don't let that scare you off! While the costs may seem high, the rewards are worth it – a career in aviation can be incredibly fulfilling and open up a world of opportunities.

Plus, many flight schools offer financing options, scholarships, and payment plans to help make training more affordable. So, while your wallet might take a bit of a hit, there are ways to manage the costs and still reach your goal of becoming a pilot. :D

Decide on Your Career Path

The first step is to decide what type of pilot you want to become. There are several different career paths in aviation, including:

- **Private Pilot:** For those who want to fly for personal reasons, without earning money.
- **Commercial Pilot:** Allows you to earn money as a pilot, flying passengers or cargo.
- **Airline Transport Pilot (ATP):** The highest level of pilot certification, required to be a captain for an airline.
- **Military Pilot:** Pilots who operate military aircraft, which usually involves training provided by the military.

Choosing your career path will help determine the type of training and licenses you need.

Educational Requirements

In many countries, a minimum level of education is required to become a pilot. Generally, this means:

- **High School Diploma (or equivalent):** Most flight schools and airlines require this as a basic qualification.

- **Strong Background in Mathematics and Physics:** Understanding aerodynamics, navigation, and other technical aspects of flying requires a solid foundation in math and science.

Some airlines may prefer candidates with a university degree, especially for more competitive positions, but it is not always mandatory.

Obtain a Medical Certificate

Before starting flight training, aspiring pilots need to pass a medical examination to ensure they are fit to fly. There are different classes of medical certificates, which determine what kind of flying activities a pilot can engage in:

- **Class 1:** Required for Airline Transport Pilots (**ATP**), the highest level of medical certification. It involves a comprehensive examination, including checks on vision, hearing, cardiovascular health, and overall physical fitness. This certification is mandatory for those aiming to become airline captains or first officers.

- **Class 2:** Required for Commercial Pilots who want to earn money for flying but are not operating as airline pilots. The examination is less rigorous than Class 1 but still ensures the pilot's health and ability to operate aircraft safely.

- **Class 3:** Required for Private Pilots and Student Pilots. It is the least stringent and covers basic health checks. This class is sufficient for those flying for leisure or beginning their training.

Pilots must renew their medical certificates periodically to ensure they maintain the necessary fitness levels for safe operation.

Enroll in a Flight School

After passing the medical exam, the next step is to choose a flight school. There are many options worldwide, ranging from small local flight schools to large, internationally recognized training academies. When selecting a flight school, consider:

- **Location:** Proximity to home, weather conditions, and air traffic at the training airport.
- **Cost:** Flight training can be expensive, so compare different schools and their fee structures.
- **Reputation and Instructors:** Research the school's success rate, facilities, and quality of instructors.

Many flight schools offer comprehensive programs that take students from zero experience to becoming a licensed commercial pilot.

Obtain a Private Pilot License (PPL)

The Private Pilot License (**PPL**) is the first step in your journey to becoming a professional pilot. The PPL allows you to fly for personal use but not for compensation. To earn a PPL, you will need to:

- Complete a minimum number of flight hours (**usually around 40-60 hours, depending on the country's regulations**).
- Pass a theoretical exam covering subjects such as navigation, meteorology, air law, and flight principles.
- Successfully complete a practical flight test with an examiner, demonstrating your flying skills.

The PPL serves as the foundation for further training and is a prerequisite for pursuing a commercial pilot license.

Build Flight Experience

After earning a PPL, aspiring commercial pilots need to log additional flight hours to gain experience. This is often referred to as time building. Some ways to build hours include:

- Renting aircraft and flying cross-country routes.
- Participating in flight clubs or aviation groups.
- Becoming a flight instructor to gain experience while teaching others.

Most countries require pilots to accumulate at least 200-250 hours before they can apply for a commercial pilot license, but these requirements may vary.

Obtain a Commercial Pilot License (CPL)

The Commercial Pilot License (CPL) allows you to be paid for flying. The requirements for obtaining a CPL typically include:

- **Completion of Ground School:** More advanced theoretical training that covers topics like advanced navigation, flight planning, and aircraft systems.
- **Additional Flight Training:** Focused on more complex maneuvers, instrument flying, and multi-engine operation.
- **Instrument Rating (IR):** An essential qualification that allows pilots to fly in various weather conditions by relying on instruments rather than visual references.
- **Night Rating:** Training to operate an aircraft safely during nighttime.

The CPL opens the door to various flying jobs, such as cargo transport, regional airlines, or private charters.

Multi-Engine Rating

Most commercial aircraft have more than one engine, so pilots need to be proficient in handling multi-engine planes. The Multi-Engine Rating is an add-on to your license that allows you to fly these types of aircraft. The training covers:

- Engine failure procedures.
- Multi-engine aerodynamics.
- Performance and emergency handling.

Obtain an Airline Transport Pilot License (ATPL)

For those aspiring to become an airline pilot, the final step is obtaining the Airline Transport Pilot License (**ATPL**). This is the highest level of certification and is required for pilots who wish to serve as captains on commercial airlines. The ATPL requirements include:

- Minimum Flight Hours: Generally, at least 1,500 flight hours are needed, including night flying, cross-country flights, and multi-engine time.
- Extensive Theoretical Exams: Covering topics like advanced navigation, meteorology, and aircraft systems.
- Simulator Training: Often conducted in sophisticated flight simulators, focusing on emergency situations, instrument failures, and other complex scenarios.

Airline Training Programs

Many aspiring airline pilots choose to apply directly to airline-sponsored training programs. These programs, often called cadet programs, provide a structured path from flight school to becoming a first officer (**co-pilot**) on an airline. They include:

- **Integrated Flight Training: Combines** all necessary training from zero hours to becoming a licensed airline pilot.
- **Job Placement:** Graduates are often placed directly into a position with the sponsoring airline, subject to successful completion of the program.

Continuous Learning and Recurrent Training

Even after becoming a licensed pilot, training does not stop. Airlines and aviation authorities require pilots to undergo recurrent training regularly to ensure their skills remain sharp. This includes:

- **Simulator Checks:** Practicing emergency procedures and abnormal scenarios.
- **Medical Examinations:** Regular health checks to maintain fitness to fly.

Renewal of Licenses and Ratings: Pilots must keep their licenses, ratings, and certifications up to date, including their instrument and multi-engine ratings.

Becoming a pilot is a challenging but rewarding journey that requires dedication, hard work, and continuous learning. By following these general steps, aspiring pilots can navigate their way through the training and certifications needed to pursue a career in aviation. Although the process may vary slightly from country to country, the fundamental requirements remain the same: passion, knowledge, and a commitment to safety.

I wish you the best of luck on your journey! Whether you're just starting out or already well on your way, I'd love to hear from you. Feel free to reach out to me on Instagram and let me know if you're working towards your pilot's license or if you've just achieved your dream of becoming a pilot.

Networking in Aviation

Networking is a crucial aspect of any profession, and aviation is no exception. Building and maintaining professional relationships can significantly enhance your career, whether you are an aspiring pilot, an aviation technician, or involved in any other sector of the industry. This chapter will explore the importance of networking in aviation, effective strategies for building connections, and tips for maintaining those relationships.

The Importance of Networking

Career Opportunities: Many job openings in aviation are filled through personal connections and referrals rather than traditional job postings. Networking allows you to tap into this hidden job market, giving you access to opportunities that you might not find elsewhere.

Knowledge Sharing: Engaging with others in the industry provides access to a wealth of knowledge and experience. Networking allows you to learn from the successes and challenges of others, which can be invaluable in your own career.

Mentorship: Building relationships with experienced professionals can lead to mentorship opportunities. A mentor can provide guidance, support, and insights that can help you navigate your career path more effectively.

Professional Development: Networking events often include workshops, seminars, and discussions that can enhance your skills and knowledge. By participating in these events, you can stay current with industry trends and best practices.

Building a Support System: The aviation industry can be demanding, and having a network of like-minded professionals can provide emotional and professional support. Sharing experiences and challenges with others in the field can create a sense of community.

Effective Networking Strategies

Attend Industry Events: Participate in aviation conferences, airshows, and trade shows. These events provide excellent opportunities to meet industry professionals, learn about new developments, and expand your network.

Join Aviation Organizations: Becoming a member of aviation associations or clubs can open doors to networking opportunities. Many organizations host events, webinars, and forums where you can connect with fellow members.

Utilize Social Media: Platforms like LinkedIn and Twitter are powerful tools for networking. Share your experiences, engage with industry content, and connect with professionals in your field. Building an online presence can help you establish credibility and attract potential connections.

Informational Interviews: Reach out to professionals in your desired field for informational interviews. This approach not only helps you learn about their career paths but also establishes a personal connection that could lead to future opportunities.

Volunteer: Offering your time and skills to aviation-related organizations or events can help you meet new people while showcasing your commitment to the industry. Volunteering is an excellent way to build relationships organically.

Vocabulary

A/C - Aircraft

ACARS - Aircraft Communications Addressing and Reporting System

ACAS - Airborne Collision Avoidance System

ADF - Automatic Direction Finder

ADI - Attitude Director Indicator

ADIRS - Air Data Inertial Reference System

AFCS - Automatic Flight Control System

AFT - After or Rearward

AGL - Above Ground Level

AHRS - Attitude and Heading Reference System

AIM - Aeronautical Information Manual

ALS - Approach Lighting System

AMSL - Above Mean Sea Level

APU - Auxiliary Power Unit

ARFF - Aircraft Rescue and Fire Fighting

ARINC - Aeronautical Radio, Incorporated

ARSR - Air Route Surveillance Radar

ARTCC - Air Route Traffic Control Center

ASDA - Accelerate-Stop Distance Available

ASR - Airport Surveillance Radar

ATC - Air Traffic Control

ATIS - Automatic Terminal Information Service

ATS - Air Traffic Services

ATPL - Airline Transport Pilot License

AWOS - Automated Weather Observing System

CAVOK - Ceiling and Visibility OK

CDI - Course Deviation Indicator

CDU - Control Display Unit

CFI - Certified Flight Instructor

CFR - Code of Federal Regulations

CG - Center of Gravity

CNS/ATM - Communication, Navigation, Surveillance/Air Traffic Management

COM - Communication

CVR - Cockpit Voice Recorder

CTA - Control Area

CTAF - Common Traffic Advisory Frequency

CTR - Control Zone

CVR - Cockpit Voice Recorder

DME - Distance Measuring Equipment

EADI - Electronic Attitude Director Indicator

EFIS - Electronic Flight Instrument System

EHSI - Electronic Horizontal Situation Indicator

EICAS - Engine Indicating and Crew Alerting System

ELT - Emergency Locator Transmitter

ETA - Estimated Time of Arrival

ETOPS - Extended-range Twin-engine Operational Performance Standards

FAF - Final Approach Fix

FBO - Fixed-Base Operator

FDR - Flight Data Recorder

FIC - Flight Information Center

FIR - Flight Information Region

FL - Flight Level

FMS - Flight Management System

FOD - Foreign Object Damage/Debris

GPWS - Ground Proximity Warning System

GPS - Global Positioning System

HAT - Height Above Touchdown

HF - High Frequency

HPA - Hectopascal

HUD - Head-Up Display

IATA - International Air Transport Association

ICAO - International Civil Aviation Organization

ILS - Instrument Landing System

IMC - Instrument Meteorological Conditions

INS - Inertial Navigation System

IRS - Inertial Reference System

ISA - International Standard Atmosphere

LAHSO - Land and Hold Short Operations

LDA - Localizer Type Directional Aid

LOC - Localizer

LNAV - Lateral Navigation

LOFT - Line-Oriented Flight Training

MDA - Minimum Descent Altitude

MEL - Minimum Equipment List

METAR - Meteorological Aerodrome Report

MLS - Microwave Landing System

MOCA - Minimum Obstruction Clearance Altitude

MRA - Minimum Reception Altitude

MSL - Mean Sea Level

NDB - Non-Directional Beacon

NOTAM - Notice to Airmen

NTSB - National Transportation Safety Board

OAT - Outside Air Temperature

PAPI - Precision Approach Path Indicator

PAX - Passengers

PIC - Pilot in Command

PIREPs - Pilot Reports

PNR - Point of No Return

QNH - Altimeter Setting to Obtain Elevation

RA - Resolution Advisory

RVR - Runway Visual Range

RVSM - Reduced Vertical Separation Minimum

SA - Situation Awareness

SAR - Search and Rescue

SIDs - Standard Instrument Departures

SIGMET - Significant Meteorological Information

SOP - Standard Operating Procedure

STARs - Standard Terminal Arrival Routes

STOL - Short Takeoff and Landing

TAF - Terminal Aerodrome Forecast

TAS - True Airspeed

TCAS - Traffic Collision Avoidance System

TFR - Temporary Flight Restriction

TMA - Terminal Control Area

TODA - Takeoff Distance Available

TORA - Takeoff Run Available

TSO - Technical Standard Order

UTC - Coordinated Universal Time

VASI - Visual Approach Slope Indicator

VFR - Visual Flight Rules

VHF - Very High Frequency

VMC - Visual Meteorological Conditions

VNAV - Vertical Navigation

VOR - VHF Omnidirectional Range

VSI - Vertical Speed Indicator

WX - Weather

Chapter 12

Special Topics and FAQs

Why Aircraft Lights are Dimmed During Takeoff & Landing?

As passengers prepare for takeoff or landing, a common safety measure is implemented: the cabin lights are dimmed. This seemingly simple action has important safety implications. In this chapter, we will explore the reasons behind dimming aircraft lights during these critical phases of flight and understand the benefits it provides.

Eye Adaptation: Dimming the lights helps passengers' and crew members' eyes adjust to the lower light levels outside the aircraft. If an emergency were to occur, the rapid adjustment to darkness ensures that everyone on board can see better outside, facilitating a quicker and safer evacuation.

Reduced Glare: Bright cabin lights can cause reflections and glare on the windows, obstructing the view of the outside environment. Dimming the lights minimizes these reflections, allowing passengers and crew to see outside more clearly and spot any potential hazards.

Emergency Lighting: In the event of an emergency, the dimmed cabin lights make the emergency lighting system more visible. This system includes illuminated exit signs and floor path lighting, which guide passengers to exits. The enhanced contrast between the emergency lights and the dimmed cabin lights ensures that these vital indicators are easily noticeable.

Preparedness for Evacuation: During an emergency evacuation, it's crucial for passengers to quickly find their way to the exits. By dimming the lights, the transition to emergency lighting is smoother, reducing panic and confusion and helping passengers navigate towards exits more efficiently.

Energy Efficiency: Dimming the cabin lights helps conserve power during takeoff and landing. This is particularly beneficial in preserving battery life for emergency systems, ensuring they are fully operational if needed.

Why Don't PLANES Have Parachutes for Passengers?

The idea of providing parachutes for passengers on commercial flights might seem like a sensible safety measure. However, there are several reasons why this is not a practical solution in the aviation industry. This chapter explores the key reasons why parachutes are not provided for passengers on airplanes.

High Altitude Challenges

Commercial airplanes typically cruise at altitudes of 30,000 to 40,000 feet, where the conditions are extremely harsh:

Thin Air

At such high altitudes, the air is very thin, making it difficult to breathe without supplemental oxygen. Parachuting from these heights would require passengers to have specialized oxygen equipment and training to use it properly.

Extreme Cold

Temperatures at cruising altitudes can drop to -40°C or lower. Passengers would need to be equipped with special suits to survive the cold, which adds complexity and weight.

Training and Physical Fitness

Parachuting safely requires significant training and physical fitness. Most passengers do not have the necessary skills or physical capability to jump from an aircraft and control a parachute, especially under emergency conditions.

Rapid Deployment

In an emergency, there is often very little time to react. The process of distributing parachutes, instructing passengers on their use, and safely deploying them from the aircraft would take valuable time that might not be available.

Safety of Egress

Jumping from a commercial airliner is extremely dangerous due to several factors:

Aircraft Speed

Commercial airplanes travel at speeds of around *500-600 miles* per hour. Exiting an aircraft at these speeds would be perilous, as the wind force alone could cause serious injury or death.

Risk of Collision

Passengers jumping from an aircraft risk colliding with parts of the plane, such as the tail or wings, as well as with other passengers. Ensuring a safe egress for a large number of people is nearly impossible.

Effective Safety Measures

Instead of parachutes, the aviation industry relies on a range of highly effective safety measures:

Advanced Technology

Modern airplanes are equipped with advanced technology for navigation, weather detection, and collision avoidance, significantly reducing the risk of accidents.

Rigorous Maintenance

Aircraft undergo strict maintenance schedules and inspections to ensure they are in optimal working condition.

Trained Crew

Flight crews receive extensive training to handle emergencies, including evacuations and first aid, ensuring passenger safety during unforeseen events.

Aircraft Communication Systems

Aircraft communication systems are the backbone of safe and efficient flight operations. They enable pilots to coordinate with air traffic control (**ATC**), receive real-time updates, and handle emergencies. From basic voice radios to advanced satellite links, these systems ensure seamless interaction between the aircraft, ground stations, and other aircraft.

Key Components of Aircraft Communication Systems

VHF (Very High Frequency) Radios:

- Purpose: Primary communication with ATC, especially within line-of-sight (**≈200 NM range**).
- Frequency Range: 118–137 MHz.
- Usage: Routine exchanges (**e.g., clearances, weather updates**), tower communication during takeoff/landing.
- Example: "Hannover Tower, DLH123, ready for departure."

HF (High Frequency) Radios:

- Purpose: Long-distance communication over oceans or remote areas.
- Frequency Range: 2–30 MHz.
- Usage: Transoceanic flights where VHF is out of range.
- Limitation: Prone to atmospheric interference.

SATCOM (Satellite Communication):

- Purpose: Global coverage, even over oceans and polar regions.
- Technology: Uses geostationary satellites (**e.g., Inmarsat, Iridium**).
- Applications: Voice calls, data transmission (**e.g., weather maps, emails**).

ACARS (Aircraft Communications Addressing and Reporting System):

- Purpose: Digital data link for text-based messages.
- Usage: Automated reports (**e.g., engine performance, position updates**), flight plan changes.
- Example: Sending "OUT" (**off-block**) and "ON" (**on-block**) messages to airlines.

Emergency Frequencies:

- 121.5 MHz: International distress frequency (**guard channel**).
- 406 MHz: Emergency Locator Transmitter (**ELT**) for crash alerts.

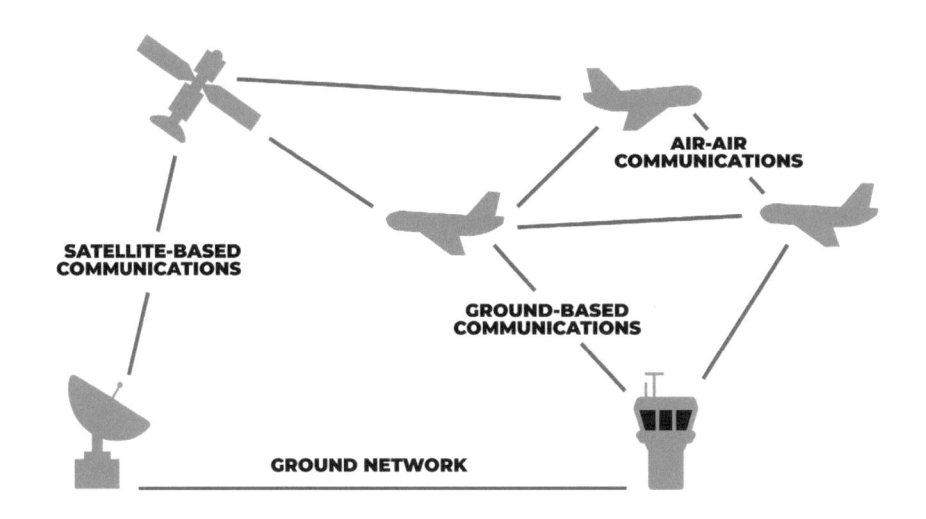

How Communication Systems Work

Voice Communication:

- Pilots use VHF/HF radios to speak directly with ATC. Standard phraseology minimizes misunderstandings (**e.g., "Wilco" for "Will comply"**).
- SELCAL (**Selective Calling**): Allows ATC to alert specific aircraft via a tone, reducing cockpit noise.

Data Communication:

- CPDLC (**Controller-Pilot Data Link Communications**): Enables text-based ATC instructions (**e.g., "CLIMB TO FL350"**).
- ADS-B (**Automatic Dependent Surveillance-Broadcast**): Shares real-time aircraft position, altitude, and speed with ATC and nearby aircraft.

Satellite-Based Systems:

- SATCOM Voice/Data: Supports clear communication in remote areas.
- FANS (**Future Air Navigation System**): Integrates SATCOM and CPDLC for oceanic routes.

Safety and Redundancy:

- Dual Systems: Aircraft carry redundant radios to ensure communication during failures.
- Priority Channels: Emergency frequencies (**121.5 MHz**) are monitored continuously.
- Encryption: Sensitive data (**e.g., military flights**) uses encrypted channels.

Modern Innovations

LDACS (L-band Digital Aeronautical Communications System):

- Upcoming European standard for secure, high-speed air-to-ground communication.

5G Aviation Networks:

- Enhances data throughput for real-time weather updates and video streaming.

AI-Powered Voice Recognition:

- Reduces pilot workload by automating routine calls (**e.g., "Request pushback"**).

Example Scenario: Oceanic Crossing

Pre-Flight:

- Pilot files a flight plan via ACARS.

En Route:

- Uses HF radio or SATCOM for position reports over the ocean.

Emergency:

- Activates ELT on 406 MHz, switches to 121.5 MHz for voice coordination with rescue teams.

Aircraft communication systems are vital for safety, efficiency, and coordination in global aviation. From analog radios to AI-driven networks, these technologies ensure pilots stay connected, whether cruising over continents or oceans. Understanding their operation prepares aviators to handle routine flights and emergencies with confidence.

Thank you for reading!

Made in United States
Troutdale, OR
03/21/2025